REVIEWS OF PLANETARY SYMBOLISM

What distinguishes this series from other astrological texts is the author's skillful cross-discipline of depth-psychology with astrology.... Planetary Symbolism is an intelligent introductory astro-psychological text that astrologers, students, and Jungians interested in astrology will value and use.

—Pat Stoyko, Above and Below

What makes this book demonstrably different from the average presentation of planet-in-sign collage is the quality of the delineations. Dr. Hamaker-Zondag's scholarship is patently obvious, her writing is lucid and easily understood, and the presentation of quite complex concepts is developed in such a way as to make it accessible to all.

—FAA Journal, Vol. 17, No. 3

Planetary Symbolism in the Horoscope

Planetary Symbolism in the Horoscope

Karen Hamaker-Zondag

SAMUEL WEISER, INC.

York Beach, Maine

Published in 1996 by
Samuel Weiser, Inc.
P. O. Box 612
York Beach, ME 03910-0612
USA

97 99 01 02 00 98 96
2 4 6 8 9 7 5 3 1

Library of Congress Catalog Card Number: 82-50535
ISBN 0-87728-868-2

Translated by Transcript, Ltd., Clevedon, England

Cover art titled "No. 1"
Copyright © 1996 Norbert Lösche/Yonca Kirkli.
Walter Holl Agency, Aachen, Germany.

Astyrological charts calculated using *Solar Fire*
from Astrolabe, Brewster, MA, USA

Typeset in 10 point Baskerville

Printed in the United States of America

For Inge Wolf

TABLE OF CONTENTS

INTRODUCTION

This book has been written after much hesitation on my part. I had no wish to write yet another collection of ready-made interpretations of the planets in the signs. It's hard to find anything particularly instructive in collections of this sort. Although there is nothing wrong with cookbook astrology it seldom forces the student to think about the symbolism of astrology. Aggression and extraversion are possibilities belonging to all Aries planetary positions, for example, but we have to cope with the placement one way when the Sun is concerned and in another when the Moon, Mars or other planets are concerned; the background influences and less obvious patterns necessitate a flexible approach. In this present volume, I have endeavored to provide this background and to show its implications as clearly as possible. Consequently, the reader will be able to use the book in several different ways:

1. As a quick guide to interpretation. I hope that nothing I have written will be used blindly! There are no cut-and-dried recipes. An analysis confined to the influences of the planets in the signs is in some respects indispensable, since it gives insight into the wants and wishes likely to be generated by the planets quite apart from their aspects, dispositorships or other factors.

2. In Appendix II, you will find a summary of the influences of the planets, the elements and the quadruplicities in key-word form.

Astrological Signs and Symbols

Sign	Symbol	Day Ruler	Night Ruler	Element	Cross
Aries	♈	Mars ♂	Pluto ♇	Fire	Cardinal
Taurus	♉	Venus ♀	—	Earth	Fixed
Gemini	♊	Mercury ☿	—	Air	Mutable
Cancer	♋	Moon ☽	—	Water	Cardinal
Leo	♌	Sun ☉	—	Fire	Fixed
Virgo	♍	Mercury ☿	—	Earth	Mutable
Libra	♎	Venus ♂	—	Air	Cardinal
Scorpio	♏	Pluto ♇	Mars ♂	Water	Fixed
Sagittarius	♐	Jupiter ♃	Neptune ♆	Fire	Mutable
Capricorn	♑	Saturn ♄	Uranus ♅	Earth	Cardinal
Aquarius	♒	Uranus ♅	Saturn ♄	Air	Fixed
Pisces	♓	Neptune ♆	Jupiter ♃	Water	Mutable

Since the signs belong both to elements and to quadruplicities, it is important to learn to combine these definitions. Hence this may be treated as an exercise book. As proficiency is gained in handling component factors (the planets, elements, and quadruplicities), there will be no further need for ready-made interpretations because the student's intuition and understanding will form the diagnosis.

3. It probably makes most sense, in training our powers of deduction, to first read what is said about the Sun in a given sign before considering any of the other planets.* By so doing, we kill two birds with one stone: in the first place, we see how the various interpretations are derived by logical reasoning, and, in the second, we gain an insight into the basic characteristics of the signs and use this background knowledge for interpreting the meanings of the other planets in the signs.

4. Finally, example charts are included in Appendix I so the reader can discover how to combine the various (and often conflicting) influences and patterns in a horoscope. The short readings, which have been made as clear as possible, can be employed as a key for solving problems arising in the synthesis of this part of horoscope interpretation. The reader may also wish to compare the material included here with that provided for these same charts in Volume 1.

The book has had its origin in lessons given to my students, and if they had not kept asking me the whys and wherefores time and time again, it would never have taken its present form. My students have helped me and I would like to share this knowledge. I wish to express my grateful thanks to my students and also to my husband Hans, who as always has devotedly read through the manuscript and has suggested numerous improvements.

Amsterdam, May, 1980

---

*The Sun is called a planet by astrologers for the sake of convenience, although we all know that the Sun and Moon are not planets.—Tr.

Planetary Symbolism in the Horoscope

CHAPTER ONE

THE PLANETS: STAGES IN THE HISTORY
OF HUMAN DEVELOPMENT

In the beginning of human evolution, the psyche was still strongly swayed by the struggle for existence. At that time man was kept busy defending himself against other forms of life, foraging for food and propagating the species. Eventually certain responses and patterns of behavior developed in the human psyche due to these prevailing biological conditions. All this condensed experience from the past is, so to speak, stored up in the collective unconscious of mankind, and is still playing a part in the human psyche in the form of archetypes.[1]

The presence of various patterns of instinctive behavior stored in the depths of the unconcious has pushed our species further and further along the road of evolution, and gradually widened the gap between ourselves and other creatures. And yet we have retained basic behavioral characteristics, although more differentiated, stemming from age-old reaction patterns and ways of acting.

The planets are the purest symbols we have for certain human motives and forms of conduct, and on the basis of the succession of the planets we can draw ourselves a picture of the possible course of development of the human species. It is perhaps easier to understand

---

[1]See my book, *Astro-Psychology*, Samuel Weiser, Inc., York Beach, ME, USA, and The Aquarian Press, Wellingborough, UK, 1980, p.139. (Now published as *Psychological Astrology*, Samuel Weiser, Inc., York Beach, ME, USA, 1989.)

the influences of the planets if we place them in historical perspective.

The Sun and Moon play a special and distinctive part in the process of development. Although they are not, strictly speaking, planets, we call them such for the sake of simplicity. The Sun is a star and the Moon is a satellite of the Earth. The influence exerted on the psyche by the Sun and Moon can best be considered as two important parts of the psyche, with the Sun being regarded as representing the center of the field of consciousness and the Moon as the symbol for the contents of the human unconscious.

However, if the psyche is to function, more is needed than the contents of the conscious and the unconscious mind represented by the Sun and the Moon. These contents come to life only when they can come in contact with one another and enter into mutual action and exchange. The conscious and unconscious can then work in conjunction and in opposition, leading to the growth and development of the individual psyche.

The planet Mercury is the symbol for our ability to communicate and combine. It is the psychic drive that causes us to make contact with one another in a neutral and nonemotional manner; it impels us to gather information and to engage in give-and-take, and so on. Through Mercury the conscious and unconscious contents of the human psyche can connect, and in bringing this about the planet is essential to development of consciousness.

Although Mercury has to do with the inner flow, backward and forward, between the conscious and the unconscious contents of the mind, its role in the world at large must not be underrated. It is the planet that brings human beings into mutual contact and links them together. Consequently, it is also the planet that enables us to mirror one another and so to experience what is contained in our own unconscious.[2]

Mercury is the planet of communication, and communication can take place in different ways; for example, by means of some attitude or gesture, or by the written or spoken word. Hence Mercury rules linguistic communication and expression. Among the other things it does, language distinguishes man from the animals: although animals can certainly convey messages to others of their

---

[2]For a clear explanation of the projection mechanism see Harding, M.E., *The I and the Not I:* A study in the development of consciousness, Princeton: 1973.

own species via sounds and/or body signals (such as are found in the complicated "language" of the bees), man is able to make his messages extremely specific—the capability of speech. Owing to its function in the human horoscope, the planet Mercury has become a symbol of great significance since the interchanges between the conscious and the unconscious minds and between the outer and inner worlds can be refined by its influence.

Shades of meaning can be further introduced by the thought processes as they connect words and concepts; we may even come to regard speech as a prerequisite for thought. Speech enables us to make sense of what we have experienced, to assimilate it and to classify it under preexisting patterns of experience. Without Mercury, the survival of our species in its present form would be inconceivable.

When primitive man became sociable and began to make contacts with his fellows, the impersonal, colorless planet Mercury was indispensable in forming the connections. We call it colorless because, although its activities suit the requirements of the moment, it lends nothing to what is taking place. It is the mediator. The other planets—or pyschic influences, if you will—are the ones which color the meaning of messages. By assimilating a range of influences, we are able to develop, to enlarge the ego and to hold our own more effectively.

From a primeval subsistence-level situation, human beings have steadily developed in the direction of individualism. During the initial period (and probably during the transition period too) of our development we were still characterized by nondifferentiation and chaos: ego-consciousness did not exist, and rational reactions were only just beginning to emerge from the instinctive ones. Since everyday life was largely governed by the struggle for existence, people were fully engaged in hunting for food, in securing a permanent base (for refuge and shelter) and in rearing a family. As Erich Neumann says:

> ...the primitive situation, mythologically represented by Ouroboros,* corresponds to that psychological stage in human prehistory in which the individual and the group, the ego and the unconscious, the inhabitant and

---

*The representation of a serpent swallowing its own tail.—Tr.

the world he inhabits are still so indissolubly bound
together that the law of "mystic participation," or of
unconscious identification prevails.[3]

"Participation mystique" means that the individual still makes no
distinction between himself and the group; he assumes that
everything that happens to himself is also happening to the group.
The individual feels involved in all the phenomena which surround
him, and enters into them emotionally—living so intimately with
nature that he tends to project all his hopes and fears into it. For
him, the trees are inhabited by spirits, he seeks to encounter the
spirits of his ancestors and so on. Everything "lives" as far as he is
concerned, everything has a soul of its own, and he himself shares in
this invisible life and must make sure to take it into account in all
kinds of possible and impossible ways. Psychologists would say that
he projected all the contents of his own unconscious on the outside
world. He is dependent on these powers which he experiences as
being outside himself, although in fact they are nothing more than
reflections of his own unconscious. In this connection, Erich
Neumann remarks that:

> ...first comes the outward, the external representation of
> a content; only in the later stages of consciousness is the
> content seen as something belonging to the psyche
> itself....The forming and unfolding of the human
> personality consists chiefly of the incorporation or
> introjection of those contents which have been imaged
> externally.[4]

And he goes on:

> ...History teaches us that, to begin with, the individual
> did not exist as an independent entity but was dominated
> by the group; the development of an independent ego not
> being permitted. We find this state of affairs in all
> sections of social and cultural life: collective anonymity
> is the order of the day.

---

[3]Neumann, E., *The Origins and History of Consciousness*, Princeton: 1969, pp. 266-267.
[4]Neumann, E., *The Origins and History of Consciousness*, Princeton: 1969, pp. 272-273.

> This original group unity did not arise from some objective group soul distinct from its members. Naturally from the very start there would have been individual differences between group members, allowing them a limited measure of independence....[5]

Therefore, we are compelled to see the individual as an organ in an independently functioning body, and not as something on his own. The group as such held the individual in a very firm grip so that the ego could only very gradually and slowly manage to escape from the tyranny of the group.

> Even though recent investigations have shown that the individual in primitive societies came quite early into conflict with the group, it is nevertheless certain that the further we go back in human history the more rarely does individuality appear and the less marked is its development.[6]

A point to bear in mind is that the safest course for men and women in those early times was to stay together in close groups. Many dangers lay in wait in nature, and by staying with the group (during a hunting expedition for example) the individual was less vulnerable. Such social ties made people stronger in the face of a hostile environment and offered them help, reassurance and security.

How does all this apply to the planets? We know that the planets can be perceived as psychic energies; the reason being that these energies have grouped themselves into a definite whole in our psyche, in one way or another, in order to function. In the course of many generations we have gradually developed stereotypes of behavior and reaction patterns for the preservation of the species. These patterns are so deeply ingrained in the human mind that they seem to be inherited, just like the instincts of animals. We instinctively seek certain circumstances and expedients because we "know" that they are best for the species. The "knowledge" is not always conscious but is a projection of an inborn (collective)

---

[5] Neumann, E., *The Origins and History of Consciousness*, Princeton: 1969, pp. 268-269.
[6] Neumann, E., *The Origins and History of Consciousness*, Princeton: 1969, p. 269.

behavior pattern. During the course of human evolution all sorts of different patterns have crystallized from experiences stored in the collective unconscious of humanity as a whole, making our race what it is today.

> These inherited unconscious behavior patterns form driving forces behind contemporary human behavior, and we see them symbolized by the planets in the conceptual framework of astrology.[7]

It should be clear by now that, as said previously, the Sun and Moon cannot function on their own. Mercury is the link binding Sun and Moon (the conscious and unconscious mind) into a dynamic working unit. At the same time, Mercury is the connection between the two psychic entities. Through neutral Mercury, different individuals come into contact with one another, and groups are formed right at the start of human history with the unconscious, mainly biological, aim of collective security. Group formation as a social act and the need for safety and comfort, however, are represented by the planet Venus.

We all have the planet Venus in our horoscope, and in each one of us there is present the primitive pattern expressed by this planet, the archetypal psychic content. But the manner in which this content expresses itself will differ from one person to another, depending on how the remainder of the horoscope is structured.

In the social communities we have been considering, it was easy for teams and friendships to be formed in keeping with the influence of the planet Venus. As time went by, however, the significance of this planet was extended from affiliations with a number of persons for the sake of comfort and safety to relationship with one persn for the sake of another sort of security. Physical security began to lose some of its urgency because mankind learned to control the environment; efficient hunting and farming methods had made subsistence more certain. The search for security became diverted to more subtle values, the emotional ones. And so Venus evolved into the planet of love, but even this love is a derivative of the original pattern that contains the search for comfort and security.

It must be said that there will always be people who do not marry for love; the most important values in marriage as far as they

[7]Hamaker-Zondag, K. M., *Astro-Psychology*, Samuel Weiser, Inc., York Beach, ME, USA, and The Aquarian Press, Wellingborough, UK, 1980, p. 140.

are concerned are comfort and security and functioning within a tightly knit group or family unit.[8] With the modern generation, this aspect seems to have been pushed rather into the background, but appearances are often deceptive. For though it is true that this psychic factor has been further developed and differentiated, it is also true that its original and most elementary forms of expression still remain with us. And these forms of expression still manifest themselves from time to time, especially in periods of personal or social crisis. In any case, we have only to look around us to see how strongly the impersonal group values survive, holding us more firmly in their grip than we might wish.

Although the influence of the group on its individual members was initially very great, each individual has character traits which are not in keeping with the generally accepted codes of behavior of the group, and these bring each one of us in conflict with the group—often without our being consciously aware of it. There seems to be something within us that craves for separate recognition. A point is reached somewhere in the history of consciousness where the individual concerned with the development of individuality no longer says, "I am compelled to..." or "There is something that requires me to..." but boldly declares: "*I* will." That is the first step on the road to the formation of a conscious ego and the first act of disengagement from the group unit and the group mind. This clear emphasis of the personality is symbolized in astrology by the planet Mars, which is the planet that makes us say "I" in the sense of thrusting ourselves into the foreground, of distancing ourselves a little from others and of adopting a defensive stance against the authorities and powers which threaten our egos.

Often one of the first ways in which individuality is experienced is through an awareness of the body. In a way, a magical relationship exists between the body and the individual. Neumann comments on it as follows:

> This magical relationship with the body is an essential
> feature of centroversion; the most primitive stage in the
> formation of a self consists in cherishing one's own body,
> and adorning and glorifying it. The phenomenon of
> tattooing, so widespread among primitive folk, shows

---

[8] Berg, Prof. Dr. J. H. van den, *Metabletica of Leer der Veranderingen* (The fundamentals of a historical psychology), Nijkerk, 1970, p. 117.

pattern, which was one of the earliest ways in which a
this particularly clearly; as does the fact of individualistic
tattooing not in harmony with the stereotyped collective
person could emphasize his individuality... in this connection we see the tendency, even today, to express
individual qualities by the physical appearance—in the
cut of man's clothes and in *haute couture*, in the
monarch's crown and in the ribbons decorating the
military chest.[9]

(By centroversion, Erich Neumann understands the innate tendency
of a whole to make a unity of its separate parts, and to synthesize
from their differences coherent systems.)[10]

In the very slow course of time, there emerged from the
unconscious mind a center of consciousness, the ego; and the energy
symbolized by Mars was an indispensable factor in the process.
However, the tremendous importance of the physical posed a new
threat to the unfolding ego: it was still dependent on biological
values.

Another type of independence went along with that of bodily
appearance and dress. The more that people began to stand on their
own two feet, the more they engaged in conscious activities;
individual creativity manifested itself, and this was a great leap
forward for mankind. Nevertheless, the group itself was menaced by
the whole process and so, therefore, was the security and well-being
of the individual and the species. A balance has to be found between
the herd instinct and the drive to set oneself apart from the group to
develop one's own identity. Religious belief has been very important
for the maintenance of that balance. In particular, rituals, sacrifices,
initiations and the like were able to give the group a sense of unity
far greater than any expression of individuality and, initially, a
sense of unity that was unassailable by any urges people may have
had to become mavericks. Astrologically speaking, the Venus-Mars
tandem is kept on the right track by the influence of the planet
Jupiter. Jupiter represents our ventures into the religious sphere, for
we reach out toward what is higher and deeper, and seek for a more
profound unity within the greater whole. Human development, and

[9] Neumann, E., *The Origins and History of Consciousness*, Princeton: 1969, p. 180.
[10] Neumann, E., *The Origins and History of Consciousness*, Princeton: 1969, p. 286.

especially the development of the conscious mind, is attended by a gradual transformation: the instinctive impulses and mechanisms being subordinated to the modifying influence of moral, social and religious factors.[11]

The evolution of ego-consciousness runs parallel with a tendency in man to make himself independent of his body, a tendency of which the ultimate expression is aceticism, denial of the world, self-flagellation, misogyny, etc. Ritual methods for ego-expansion are employed at initiation ceremonies for adolescents. These ceremonies are designed to test the candidate's powers of endurance; they serve to increase the stability of his ego, to fortify his willpower and to "make him more of a man." They give a conscious sense of superiority over the body.[12] The rituals include the imparting of secret knowledge, and are redolent of what is superhuman, metaphysical, spiritual and cosmic. Apparently, the sharing of knowledge is a stronger bond than the mutual search for safety. The latter, of course, is represented by Venus. Originally, Venus held sway over all the norms and values—relationships within the group, social customs and the like—but purely and simply in the interests of preserving existence. Through the interposition of Jupiter (man's spiritual and religious needs) a new dimension was added, and social norms and values with a strong religious basis came into being. Faith, and its attendant dogmas, rituals, prohibitive regulations and codes of conduct, was the most important factor in channeling the aggression of Mars.[13] The splitting of the human psyche into a conscious and an unconscious marked the emergence of the ego from the womb of the "Great Mother" (the unconscious mind) into a position of self-reliance. Willpower and self-control were now important for holding instinctive drives in check.

Instead of having a sense of unity with everything around, man felt himself to be a clearly defined entity. Somewhere along the line, he was part of the larger scheme of things but, in the main, he was independent and perhaps a little lonely. Everything he encountered

[11]Hamaker-Zondag, K. M., *Astro-Psychology*, Samuel Weiser, Inc., York Beach, ME, USA, and The Aquarian Press, Wellingborough, UK, 1980, p. 159.
[12]Neumann, E., *The Origins and History of Consciousness*. Princeton: 1969, p. 310.
[13]Hamaker-Zondag, K. M., *Astro-Psychology*, Samuel Weiser, Inc., York Beach, ME, USA, and The Aquarian Press, Wellingborough, UK, 1980, p. 160.

was investigated, and analysis and differentiation were the means by which the conscious ego gained a clearer understanding of the immense concourse of facts perceivable in the outside world.

We have now reached the point where the process of becoming conscious began. On the one hand, the individual sensed the contrast between himself and the outside world, and, on the other hand, he was aware of the various urges within him as they strove for expression: of the drive to act aggressively (Mars), of the drive to find security (Venus), and of the drive to commune with a spiritually and religiously oriented world (Jupiter). The experience of pleasure and pain in this inner and outer striving insured the development of genuine consciousness.[14]

In preserving his individuality, man holds his own by continually exercising a choice between the urges struggling for expression within and by arbitrating in the conflict of the inner with the outer world. Not for nothing is Saturn (representing as it does the process of becoming conscious as choices are made and circumstances are faced) thought of as the planet of "learning by bitter experience."

The eventful journey to self-consciousness—under Saturn—has taught mankind that it is no good blaming dead ancestors or evil spirits or the like for everything that goes wrong in life when we should really be blaming ourselves. We have learned that there is a law of cause and effect which we have to understand and obey; personal responsibility has been achieved and a sense of standards. We have come to see that, to a certain extent, we can decide our own fates without reference to all sorts of outside imaginary powers.

And so, human consciousness has passed through many phases. Primitive men huddled together for safety and mutual aid. They inhabited a magical world full of mythological beings. Yet, side by side with the urge to herd together there was the urge to break away. This awakened a new, and previously dormant, desire: the desire for some spiritual or religious satisfaction. The function of Jupiter was to elevate the Venus and Mars polarity to another level. However, the conflict between Venus, Mars, and now Jupiter, forced man to keep on choosing—Saturn—a process by which man arrived at the position in which we find him today: that of a "being" who weighs

---

[14]Hamaker-Zondag, K. M., *Astro-Psychology*, Samuel Weiser, Inc., York Beach, ME, USA, and The Aquarian Press, Wellingborough, UK, 1980, p. 162.

things, makes decisions and acts on them—all the while imbued with a sense of his own importance.

There is another way of looking at the human development process. The three basic factors determining human life are:

a) the external world with all that goes on in it outside the individual, over which he has no final control;

b) the community with its interpersonal relationships;

c) the psyche as the world of the inner life.

Man has to cope with all three "worlds," and individual development depends on the way in which we do so.

For prehistoric man the worlds were more or less united, because he unconsciously shared in all three—the *participation mystique*. But to the extent that he developed as an individual, the outer world became less significant, and less threatening. Primitive man projected his unconscious mental components into everything that went on around him; but those who came after him gradually became more wary of doing so, and the contents of the unconscious mind, when they were projected, were usually projected on people. There was no conscious awareness of this as yet, but images buried deep in the unconscious were transferred unwittingly to living, tangible persons; the innate female image (the anima) for instance would be projected by a man on his wife.

Even in our own day and age, the projection of images from the unconscious on other persons still plays an important role; now, however, there is an extra dimension. With the advent of depth psychology we are coming to realize that all the characteristics we ascribe to others are reflections of our own unconscious. We behold our own psyches evidently mirrored in the outer world, in people and/or things. This mirroring process is, of course, very revealing of what occurs in the unconscious mind. A revolution has taken place in our understanding of the field of experience: what is outside ourselves is now being brought inside to its point of origin, where it belongs.

The flood of fresh insights into our own natures means that further refinements can be applied to the development of consciousness—astrologically symbolized in its various stages by the planets. Also, we are still hard at work further developing our response patterns and reshaping our consciousness.

So, for example, Venus was originally the principle in man that linked him with everything around him. The willingness to help and the love so typical of Venus embraced not only the visible world but also nature spirits and the shades of ancestors, since these were all part of the outer scheme of things and not obviously under human control.

Then, with improved insight, it was seen that there was little sense in looking for love, comfort and security in the outside world if no attempt was made to develop these qualities in the inner being. True harmony comes when we encourage in ourselves those things for which we are searching in the world. Some insight into the way in which consciousness evolves and into the relationship between inner and outer enables individuals to achieve further refinements of this point and therefore to grow, even though "growing pains" are involved.

Nevertheless, earlier forms of planetary influence have survived side by side with the newer and more sophisticated forms. Especially in times of national or personal crisis, these more elementary forms of influence can reassert themselves either to snatch us out of trouble or else to push us deeper into it—all according to circumstances and to the way in which they happen to manifest. The planets (as far out as Saturn) have helped to develop the socially well-adjusted individual—one capable of accepting responsibility and only reacting by blind instinct as a last resort.

Until late in the eighteenth century the known planets ended with Saturn and, in keeping with the development possible under the seven classical planets, man had evolved into a tolerably "well-rounded" individual who had learned to function in an increasingly complex social environment. That was the picture when, toward the close of that century, Uranus was discovered and then, within an historically short space of time, Neptune and Pluto. Suddenly fresh vistas opened up and new factors began to emerge from the unconscious so that, ever since, human evolution has proceeded rapidly. For this reason we should hesitate to assume that there are no new planets waiting to be discovered as and when yet other factors get ready for release from the unconscious into the conscious mind. Such factors as are represented by the last three (trans-saturnian) planets do not burst on the scene as things totally foreign to the human race, but have always been potentially present waiting for their day of revelation.

The recently discovered planets, having been known to us for only a short while, still contain much that is hidden, so that we are yet in the very early stages of learning how they act, what they signify and in what ways we can best respond to them. Naturally, we can deduce their action to some extent from historical trends since their discovery and from the horoscopes of those who have these planets situated at sensitive points. But this is not to say everything implied by them is immediately available to us. Just as it took early man many generations to express Venus as the impulse within that craved comfort and safety, so at the present time man is allowing both favorable and unfavorable influences from the transsaturnian planets to express themselves quite indiscriminately. These planets are impersonal. In the centuries in which we are now living they are forming their patterns of instinctive behavior. Future generations will be able to modify the patterns.

The interpretation of these planets in the horoscope does not depend, as is the case with the other planets, on thousands of years' experience. Here we have new forms and new (or renewed) psychic contents, calling for astrology to adjust and develop. We simply must not look on astrology as a static, old, or outmoded discipline, but as something dynamic and progressive keeping pace with the development of the human psyche.

The demarcation of the ego, as symbolized by Saturn, can occur in either a balance or an unbalanced fashion. One of the most important mechanisms for strengthening and enlarging the ego is the incorporation of the images of external objects or persons, a process known to psychologists as *introjection*. With the emergence of deeper and more comprehensive factors in man (heralded by the discovery of the planets Uranus, Neptune and Pluto), the saturnian process of becoming conscious can be extended into transpersonal areas. To begin with, man experiences these transpersonal forces outside himself and not till later recognizes them as parts of his own psyche and becomes able to assimilate them. When development takes place harmoniously, the problems are few: all that happens is an enrichment of the ego and of the rest of the psyche. But where there is lack of harmony, as is often the case, the assimilation process can entail considerable dangers. These should not be underestimated for they lie at the heart of many of the problems besetting us today.

In the course of achieving self-conscious awareness, man avails himself of analysis and logic and of increasingly sophisticated skills for making sense of his environment. But this can create such a gap between the conscious and the unconscious that the psyche as a whole suffers damage. The conscious and the unconscious should complement one another and, by interacting, give us an opportunity for balanced growth. If the two psychic systems become alienated, the well from which consciousness is drawn, so to speak, dries up. The unconscious stream is prevented from flowing freely, and what symbols and images it carries on its bosom to the conscious mind are ignored by the latter. Warning dreams, for example, are either misinterpreted or repressed. When an individual withdraws fully into the world of the unconscious (the very world from which the conscious mind has issued), he loses his potential for further harmonious development. In fact, a one-sided development of the conscious mind can give rise to two sorts of reaction:

a) either a neurotic personality is developed, in which compulsive acts, anxieties rising out of the unconscious, and the like, impinge disturbingly on everyday life;

b) or a kind of obsession takes over. The ego tries to nourish itself on all sorts of spiritual elements (based on archetypes) which are (still) too much for it to assimilate, and so loses touch with reality. This loss of firm ground to stand on is in this case often associated with loss of contact with the "feminine" side of life: feeling and emotion are suppressed. The individual responds to the transpersonal forces as if they restricted him to a small part of the personal ego, and the more comprehensive outlook is rejected and banished to the unconscious to work there.

As Erich Neumann puts it:

> This breaking away from the unconscious leads, on the one hand, to an ego-life without meaning and, on the other hand, to an activation of the deeper layers of the unconscious which, having been made destructive, lay waste the autocratic empire of the ego with transpersonal

invasions, collective epidemics and mass psychoses. For the disruption of the compensatory relationship between the conscious and the unconscious is not something to be taken lightly.[15]

The transsaturnian planets (Uranus, Neptune and Pluto) symbolize the new transpersonal contents of the psyche, which man must seek to integrate in his conscious mind—a process that will surely take many generations to complete. Once again, humanity seems to be at the crossroads. As we have seen, there came a time in prehistory when group members realized that they were separate entities, and each one asked himself or herself, "Who am I?" Owing to the desire to fathom the nature of his being and the nature of the struggle between his internal drives and his place in the external world, each individual developed his own ego and personally discovered the law of cause and effect. This precipitated a crisis: he himself was responsible and must learn to know his limitations. At every false step, he was liable to be overwhelmed by what was lurking in the unconscious and to suffer the loss of his hard-won ego, which had only just been drawn out of the depths of the unconscious mind. Nevertheless, mankind survived this test and reached the point where it was firmly in the saddle.

But then came a fresh crisis—a period that is not yet over. The split between matter and form, between unconscious and conscious, now threatens to become too great. Man now risks being engulfed by counterattacks from the unconscious led by the psychic influences of the newly discovered planets.

This widening gap and differentiation have pushed the development of the ego in the direction of a fragmented individualism that has lost its sense of unity. Also the original group relationships are not what they used to be in our Western society; we still talk about "the masses" but without any real emotional involvement. Old archetypal links have been broken and mankind has fallen prey to iconoclastic forces at work in the unconscious. We no longer honor God, president* or country as we once did, but fight for abstract concepts such as "work," "wealth," and "power," and, in serving these impersonal factors, we have less individuality than when we were ready to sacrifice ourselves out of piety.

---

[15]Neumann, E., *The Origins and History of Consciousness*, Princeton: 1969, p. 389.
*The Dutch version says "King." Tr.

Concentration on the conscious mind, with its penchant for the abstract and for the idea rather than the symbol, with its glorification of logic at the expense of emotion, is just as liable to precipitate a disintegration of the personality as is a direct but fruitless struggle for self-advancement. If proof were needed, we might remember the ease with which public opinion can be swayed in support of causes connected with wealth, politics, power or some strange "ism." Modern man, who has turned back to collectivism (though in a new way), has not only lost personal individuality but, due to "mass-mindedness," poses a threat to the individuality of others. This extremism can be traced to the influence of the newly discovered planets. It can lead to large-scale destruction. However, if the forces can be satisfactorily assimilated by a balanced development of the ego, many admirable transpersonal values will find expression through these planets; their influence on human abilities, on thought and feeling, on mental powers and insights may yet raise us to new heights.

By viewing the planets in the light of the evolution of man and of his conscious mind we become aware that they correspond to deep, archetypal elements of the mind. This makes them easier to understand. On reading elsewhere that the planets represent certain "principles" and energies, many will be inclined to ask, "Why these, and no more or less?" The best way to answer this question is by using the historical approach. The planets mirror in the heavens the well-worn paths in the psyche—the common experience of our race, which has made us what we are and is present in each of us in the form of the archetypes described by C. G. Jung. However, each of us gives expression to these in our own way.

From the most primitive to the most highly evolved of these archetypes we can say of them that they lie stored in our minds as instinctive reaction patterns. What this means is that they will make themselves felt when the appropriate situation calls them forth. As the distillation of all human experience through countless centuries, the planets as symbols contain a wealth of possibilities for both good and ill in human behavior. And the odds for good or ill seem evenly distributed.

CHAPTER TWO

MODES OF PLANETARY EXPRESSION

1. PRELIMINARY REMARKS

Planets reflect certain general reaction patterns of the human psyche. As Karl Kühr has so ably described it:

> In each one of us there are forces in operation corresponding to cosmic forces. Hence we are not to suppose that any planet in the sky is directly responsible for what happens to us or to our immediate environment; rather it is the power within us that harmonizes with the planet, it is *that* power which does whatever is done.

> Let us not think that Mars up above makes us disorganized; no, the corresponding force within us causes us to waste our talents by frittering them away. Schiller, with his: "...In your own character you carry with you your fateful stars..." thought to refute astrology, but was simply expressing our psychological understanding of it![16]

In psychological terms, it is best if we treat the planets as specific expressions of inner response patterns. Each planet is characterized by its own "attitudes" and "behavior," or, as we would prefer to say: each planet has certain properties uniquely its own, and these make

---

[16]Kühr, E. C., *Psychologische Horoskopdeutung:* Analyse und Synthese, Vol. 1, Vienna, 1948, p. 135.

it possible to discover in the multiplicity of human activities, postures, actions and reactions, clearly defined patterns which may be attributed to a single archetype.

The various archetypal elements can find expression both in the most elementary and in the most recondite and differentiated form within the ensemble of behavior and reactions, depending on the situation in which an individual finds himself and on his personal development. In addition to the fact that a single archetypal element can express itself with varying degrees of emphasis, there is also the fact that there are twelve different "manners" of expression open to it. On the one hand we have the twelve manners (analogous to the twelve signs of the zodiac) in which a planetary influence can work, but, on the other hand, we must also consider that *how* the influence works ranges all the way from primitive/archaic to extremely differentiated.

In studying a horoscope, it is very hard to decide whether the said influence is going to reveal its primitive or its differentiated side. The opinion frequently aired that planets making "bad" (or rather, "difficult") aspects have bad effects does not seem to hold up in the light of the experience of psychologically oriented astrologers, even though there is a grain of truth in this traditional rule. Many difficult aspects (such as squares, oppositions or inconjuncts) in a person's horoscope still do not mean that he is an evil-doer or someone who will be dogged by ill luck; it may be so, but sometimes the reverse will be true. Often the very strength of a heavily stressed horoscope will help an individual to strike out on his own, away from the beaten track, and enable him to develop according to less conventional patterns. As much may be achieved by the "afflicted" person as by one blessed with the traditionally harmonious horoscope full of trines and other easy aspects. Although this volume does not address the effects of aspects in the horoscope, it is nevertheless important to make it clear here and now that the native with many difficult aspects must not be thought of as cursed with "bad planets."

Planetary influences are psychic influences which tend to *express* something. We say "something" advisedly, because a given planet placed in a given sign does not predestine the individual (to express some fixed and unchangeable aspect of character) but, rather, signifies that a pattern of planetary influence, colored by the mode of expression of the sign in which the planet is placed, strives to *express itself and to make itself known* in a certain way. We are not trying to suggest that there is any conscious will or desire involved here, but simply that there are factors which are part of our unconscious minds, and that we instinctively feel most at one with ourselves when our behavior matches the patterns inherent in those internal factors. Patterns expressed by the difficult aspects may incline us to do things which set us at odds with society; yet, although they can present us with problems, they will often endow us with the energy and the creative thrust to overcome those problems.

In fact we have no brief for saying to anyone: "Your character reading is so-and-so." That is far too bald a statement. It is better to say: "You have such-and-such tendencies in you and these tendencies can make themselves felt in such-and-such ways." And let us remember that their modes of expression can be so varied. Take any planet in any sign: who knows whether the combined influence will manifest itself in a primitive or in a highly developed form? If in doubt, we do well to give the inquirer the whole range of possibilities, while stressing that although all are present in the planetary influence, not all will express themselves openly either at the current time or in the future. However, some of the patterns indicated by the planet will decidedly be present in the character. What is more, it is entirely possible that although certain tendencies are present in the character they have had no chance to show themselves due to repressive factors elsewhere in the horoscope or in the life circumstances, etc. However, these tendencies may suddenly assert themselves in their purest form. Whether this happens in youth or in old age is not the question here; what is in question is that at some stage or other, when the repressive mechanism has lost its usefulness or its force, an entirely unexpected facet of character can come to light.

Now for a real-life example. An astrologer was once consulted by a timid twenty-five-year-old man. The young man had never plucked up the courage to go out with a girl, and he was very unsure of himself overall. However, he did have a conjunction of Venus and Mars in Aries, which (as we shall see later) makes falling head-over-heels in love a distinct possibility. From time to time he felt consuming passions flare up inside him, but they were soon extinguished. But Mars in its own sign lent him sufficient energy to set out to make conquests, and he would make plans to sweep some young lady off her feet, although he never actually got around to doing it. Some years later the astrologer met the client again. The shy young man was much altered—he now had a reputation among his friends as a "skirt-chaser." It would take us too far afield at this point to consider how much his behavior was overcompensation for what he had had to miss in his earlier years; a close study of the whole horoscope would be required to tell us the answer. Nevertheless, it seems clear that a buried pattern strove to surface at a given moment. The way it surfaced could have been different of course, so that instead of chasing women he could have been incited by his (hyper-) active Mars in Aries to advocate alternative life styles such as open marriage, free love, a relationship with each partner retaining full independence and following his or her own career, and so on. Venus in Aries, too, would favor emancipation of the sexes. Although all these possibilities are latent in this one planetary combination, it is extremely difficult to predict which of them will come to the fore. What is more, it is entirely possible that the mode of expression will change more than once in a single lifetime. The individual has not been drastically altered; he is still expressing the same pattern. All he has done is to give it a different form, which is still in keeping with the astrological data however! That one form is socially more acceptable than another is scarcely significant. What is, in fact, true is that an individual is not necessarily "improved" by learning to be a conformist in the society in which he lives. In himself he remains the same; that he has become adaptable is a gain from the social point of view, but from another point of view he has given up access to a wealth of potential character traits and modes of expression.

That practitioners of astrology who say "*This* is what you are like" often hit the nail on the head is due to the fact that the influences often have a "preferred form of expression"—not so much because these are inherent in the influences as because they are socially determined or evoked by the environment. Many astrologers now hold the opinion that the social and general milieu in which a person lives have to be considered quite apart from the horoscope. Perhaps an example will make this clear. A girl who is a member of a central African tribe, who has the same horoscope as a girl living in the West who later makes it as a film star, is not likely to become a film star in her own social setting. Yet the pattern will tend to express itself in an equivalent fashion, and it would be no surprise if the African girl became a popular lady among her own tribespeople.

To continue: What we have to look for in a horoscope are the particular patterns seeking expression, provided the individual wishes to be himself and to develop to the best of his ability in harmony with his own personality. However, the horoscope says nothing about the level of expression or about social acceptability. And, when we are talking about the pressures exerted by society, we have also to take into account the era in which the subject lives or lived. Owing to historical progress, it is in some respects easier in present-day society to express given energies or patterns in a more satisfactory manner for the psychology of the individual. Consider the horoscope of a woman living at the turn of the century, with a powerful constellation of the energetic and intense planets Mars, Uranus and Pluto. In the period in which she lived, she would probably have displayed symptoms of hysteria, simply because there were no easy outlets for her tensions. Society made demands on her which were not in keeping with her nature. In those days, hysteria was a well-known phenomenon, since women of this type had no means of discharging their trapped energies other than hysterical outbursts. Nowadays, on the other hand, such women have the freedom to release their tension, aggression and energy in a much more satisfactory fashion. They can march in demonstrations, fight passionately for the emancipation of women, devote themselves to feminism or for environmental protection or for any other cause in which they are able to become emotionally involved and into which they can channel their energies. With their abilities, they can accomplish much as champions of women's rights, etc. The same basic influences are a work but in another direction—although once in a while they may still manifest themselves in fits of hysteria.

As astrologers, we may decide to solve the problem by listing all sorts of character traits possible with given planetary positions, but in many instances it makes better sense to take a look at the background. By looking at a person's background, we see the area that the planetary influence has to cover and can make a far better assessment of what it is likely to do, even though we can never say that a particular form of expression is fated. When due allowance has been made for horoscope data and for social, environmental and historical factors, a natal horoscope still leaves plenty of room for its components to express themselves in a number of different ways. Here lies one of the reasons why attempted character readings sometimes misfire. Nothing is so clear-cut as the recipe books, with their potted interpretations for signs, aspects and houses, would have us believe. In every case, it is the underlying pattern that is ultimately important.

2. PREDISPOSING PATTERNS

If we think back for a moment to the first chapter, we shall remember that it was suggested there that instead of being arbitrary principles thought up by man in the dim past, the planets are representatives of specific archetypal reaction patterns found in each of us, which are striving for expression. It is only the way in which these patterns come to the surface that differs from individual to individual.

It has also become clear that we must not interpret the placements of the planets as if, for example, everyone with the Sun in Aries has to be a pioneer. The more sensible approach is to say that the Sun in a given sign indicates the most natural path for an individual's ego to take, because deep down the ego experiences a need to manifest itself in that way. In other words, we are talking about urges rather than about compulsions. In "popular" astrology we keep hearing the same old stuff about the Aries person being quick-tempered and energetic, about Taurus folk being calmness itself, and about Geminis deafening the neighborhood with their chatter. Yet the Ram is sometimes quiet and composed, the Bull talkative, and the Twins taciturn, and so on. Usually, we have to look elsewhere in the horoscope to discover with what degree of ease the native can exhibit the influence of the Sun. The Sun is best thought of as our true path if we wish for optimum development of our (psychic though not necessarily social) potential. Other things being equal, it offers us the equipment for this optimum development.

The Moon represents a completely different desire pattern. When we look up the key words in handbooks we usually find that there is hardly any difference between what is said for the Sun and what is said for the Moon, except that under the heading "Moon" we read references to the feelings and emotions. If we stay with Aries for a moment, the Sun in Aries gives the pioneering spirit, it gives a continual need for new (or apparently new) things; but so does the Moon in Aries. Perhaps more feeling is involved, but someone with the Moon in Aries can make as good a pioneer as someone with the Sun in Aries. On the surface there is no obvious difference, but there is a very big difference under the surface. The Sun is of the essence of things—it is the ego. A pioneering Sun in Aries is thus in harmony with itself (but note that in giving this example we are considering only one of the possibilities of Aries expression). The Moon, on the other hand, represents conditioned, unconscious response patterns and, in practice, reveals the state in which we unconsciously feel good and in which we seek protection so to speak. It is also a state with which we can quickly (though unconsciously) identify, and this state can sometimes strongly differ from that typical of the Sun. Whenever we are in a situation where we feel uncertain and ill at ease, our "Moon behavor" comes quickly to the fore and thrusts aside that of our essential self, our Sun. If we simply say that "both Sun and Moon bestow pioneering inclinations when in Aries" we are missing a significant point, namely that whereas the Sun bestows these inclinations by virtue of its essential nature and by virtue of its natural disposition to express that nature in this way, the Moon displays the property only as habitual reactions or habitual behavior linked with the instinct to look for safety in situations which are insecure. The Moon's influence is not so steady as that of the Sun, but owing to the fact that the Moon so rapidly takes over in uncertain (and therefore in threatening or seemingly perilous) situations, individuals can have a strong emotional identification with the Moon. Conflicts between the Sun and Moon can give a person the feeling of being two different people inhabiting the same body. They need not be severe conflicts like those involving squares and oppositions; incompatible elements may also be involved. Maybe the difference between Sun and Moon signs can best be epitomized as follows: Irrespective of the level of expression, the Sun IS the sign in which it stands, and the Moon BEHAVES AS IF it were the sign in which it stands.

This explains why the Moon in a sign is more vulnerable than the Sun there. Especially in certain combinations or in certain situations, the Moon person may run into problems on this account. For instance, in a group where someone has the Sun in Leo and someone else the Moon in Leo, the one with the Sun in Leo will often expect to have a central position as a natural right and as an inherent part of the life style; what is more, this person will probably experience little difficulty in obtaining it. However, if there is any uncertainty in the group, the person with the Moon in Leo will try to cope with the situation by taking the center of the stage. It is less easy to succeed in this position than for someone with the Sun in Leo, and therefore fundamental external and/or internal conflicts can arise. If the person with the Moon in Leo is to be successful in such situations there must be indications of leadership elsewhere in the horoscope.

Obviously the Moon is a very important factor. Although it is the Sun that, symbolically as well as literally, bathes all the planets in light and makes us aware of them, it is the Moon that mirrors those reactions of ours which seem so self-evident to us, and thus is an important factor in our contact with the outside world. Now if the signs in which the Sun and Moon are placed are disparate, the native's reactions in unsure circumstances will be surprisingly different from what might have been expected from one with that Sun sign, and we say "He is not what he seems." Thus a Gemini native with the Moon in Scorpio is likely to keep quiet and say nothing in an unfamiliar situation in order to see "which way the cat jumps," only to talk nonstop about his own "mysteriousness" as soon as matters have been resolved. The Moon reaction comes first, and then that of the Sun.

3. HINTS ON INTERPRETATION

A classical rule of astrological interpetation is as follows:

> The planets always express according to the sign in which they are placed.

To put it more simply: In the first place, a planet always retains its own influence—Mercury, for instance, being always the planet of thought, contacts and connections. But, in the second place, the way in which a planet makes itself felt is indicated by the sign in which it is posited. Thus people with Mercury in Aries have the urge to express themselves on the spur of the moment—pointedly and with fire—they are quick thinkers and make contacts quickly though often not for long, etc. On the other hand, those with Mercury in Taurus have the need to make sure they get their thoughts straight before they speak; they like time to reflect, and enter into liaisons with caution. In each of these examples Mercury stands for thinking and interrelationships: it is the mode of expressing them that differs. However, the sign tells us nothing about the quality of the expression. A cautiously thinking Mercury in Taurus may be acting on the principle "more haste, less speed" or he may be slow because he is lazy. It must also be borne in mind that what we glean from the sign position of a planet is only a first approximation of the way in which the said planet will express itself; aspects, house placement, dispositorships and so on also exercise an influence.

Now, as much as the signs form the background against which we must view the planets, they themselves are combinations of the elements and crosses, and in such a way that the three signs belonging to a given element each belong to a different cross, and the four signs belonging to cross each have a different element. So crosses and elements overlap in various ways to produce twelve distinct signs, each of them unique in character. These, as we have said, are the settings in which the planets display their energies.

In the following chapters the planets will be analyzed for each of the elements. Various interesting points should become clear in the course of the analysis too. When Mars is in the element fire, it is clearly able to manifest in keeping with its own nature, yet what it is able to do in the inner and outer world is totally different for each of the three fire signs. Each of them belongs to a different cross, and it is the crosses[17] which decide *what* happens and *how* it happens. A brief example may help to clarify this. The Mars tendency toward activity easily comes out in the fire sign Aries, and the tendency is so plain because Aries is not just a fire sign; it also belongs to the cardinal cross, in which a fire sign would be most strongly oriented to the outside world. Mars in Leo is no less active, but for someone with this position the Mars energy will be felt much more strongly internally, and the actions flowing out of the Martian energy pattern will, in this individual, have repercussions on his internal and unconscious life (Leo belongs to the fixed cross), so that the Mars force is toned down in its outward expression. Alternatively its action may be delayed only to burst out with greater violence.

Anyone who has gained insight into the composition of the signs, planets, elements, and crosses, will not experience difficulty in making combinations which explain why a certain planetary position works in such and such a way. It is by no means good enough to read how Mars in Aries expresses itself, how Mars in Taurus expresses itself and so on. That sort of study does not teach

---

[17]As in Volume 1 in this series, when the author refers to the cardinal, fixed, or mutable crosses, she means the signs of the natural zodiac. This term should not be confused with the American usage of a "fixed cross," which refers to an actual aspect. Pub.

us enough about underlying motives and drives, and cannot help solve problems involving planetary expression. It is not the knowledge that Mars in Aries tries to take the world of appearances by storm that will assist us further, but the knowledge that it develops a specific urge to try and take the world by storm. For this planet (and therefore for a certain part of the psyche) it is a necessity to be able to function in this way, no matter what the outside world might think about it. On the other hand, a Mars in Leo will find that he is confronted with his own unconscious by the activity pattern that arises (Leo being a fixed sign, the influences of planets found within its borders are regressive). The desire to get on in the world often said to be typical of people with Mars in Leo is necessary for them and it enables them to face themselves regardless of whether or not the world respects or understands their achievements. Behind the external forms in which the planets express themselves there is a world of psychic processes of which we have scarcely any conception. As it happens, these psychic processes are the very things it is important for us to know, even if it be only to gain some understanding of the enormous variety of human motives and desires, learning abilities, and skills. We shall then come to see that each one of us is compelled to express ourselves and to face up to ourselves in different ways, and that we have different ways of viewing and assimilating our experiences. Astrology is no longer confined to the diagnosis of likely character traits; it has become a dynamic discipline because of the insight into the psychic processes underlying character traits that it can provide.

4. PERSONAL AND IMPERSONAL PLANETS

When interpreting the planets it is most important to differentiate between personal and impersonal planets, as we did in *Elements and Crosses as the Basis of the Horoscope.** The Sun, Moon and Mercury are completely personal, and we can clearly recognize the way in which these planets express themselves in each individual. Venus and Mars are personal, too. The "personality value" of the planets then gradually tapers off. Jupiter and Saturn are transitional; their personality value is less, but their background—the signs—still crops up in the character in certain forms.

---

*The first volume of this series, now published with the third volume of the series, *The Houses and Personality Development*, in one volume: *Foundations of Personality*, Samuel Weiser, Inc., York Beach, ME, USA, 1994.

As for the transsaturnian planets Uranus, Neptune and Pluto, these affect whole generations. They stay long in a sign and so provide the same background influence to everybody born during the years they are in a given sign. The fact that they are impersonal does not mean that these planets have no other part to play. On the contrary—their impersonal nature derives from the fact that they are strongly bound up with the human unconscious; hence the conscious mind finds them unpredictable. Certainly, they are present in every chart, and every chart belonging to a given generation has them posited in the same sign, but there are differences of house position and aspects from other planets in individual cases so they affect our personal interests and affairs to some extent. However, our main concern in this volume is sign interpretation, and this is rather difficult when it comes to the three transsaturnian planets, since their influence in the signs is purely collective in character.

5. SUMMARY

The foregoing can be summed up in a few simple statements.

1. The planets represent given psychic factors.

2. Planets form predisposing patterns which we try to release from inside us into the outside world.

3. Predisposing patterns can express themselves in many different ways.

4. It is not possible to gather from the horoscope at what level the predisposing pattern will manifest itself.

5. Besides possessing a horoscope, each individual functions within a certain environment, in a certain era and in a certain social setting.

6. The energies of the planets do not produce fixed character traits but have several possible modes of expression open to them.

7. The way in which a given planet manifests itself is determined by the sign in which it is placed.

8. Each sign can be broken down into an element and a cross.

9. The planet in an element shows the way in which that part of the psyche relates to the internal and external worlds.

10. The planet in a cross shows the method of assimilation: the way in which experiences and psychic processes are integrated into the psyche.

11. The planets preserve their qualities in all circumstances; it is only the mode of expressing these qualities that is determined by the signs.

12. A distinction must be made in interpretation between personal and impersonal planets. The personal planets are character-forming; the impersonal ones have a more collective significance.

13. The personal planets are the Sun, Moon, Mercury, Venus and Mars.

14. Jupiter and Saturn occupy an intermediate position.

15. The impersonal planets are Uranus, Neptune and Pluto.

CHAPTER THREE

PLANETS IN THE ELEMENT FIRE

In the following section we shall be studying the combinations of the planetary influences (foreground) with the influences of the elements and crosses (background). These combinations are summarized in Appendix II. While every effort will be made to avoid unnecessary repetition in the exposition, some points will have to be raised more than once for the sake of clarity.

1. CARDINAL FIRE: ARIES

SUN IN ARIES

The desire for self-realization consorts well with the cardinal cross. The fire signs, with their ardor, spontaneity and impulsiveness, cry out to be projected into the external world that has such a close relationship with the cardinal cross. The type of consciousness associated with Aries is always ready to encounter impulses from outside without modifying its behavior. The unaccommodating approach is motivated by the strong ego-involvement of the fire signs. Actually, it is not quite correct to say there is no modification: the native with the Sun in Aries does in fact—and this is a rather subtle point—modify his consciousness to the external world in the sense that his environment, the people around him and the society in which he lives create the vital and indispensable conditions for the development of his consciousness. Nevertheless, the element fire is so absorbed in itself that the only point of view it recognizes is its own. The manner in which Aries subjects measure up to their environment is as much an attempt to adapt their consciousness to the outside world as it is a search for harmony. But, be that as it may, it is invariably the outside world that engages their attention.

Aries subjects must approach the world as typical fire sign people. They assimilate their experiences in it by actively engaging in the world's work and by accepting constant input from what is going on around them. Fire tends to turn its attention on itself, and is spontaneous, warm, vital, vivacious, cheerful and loyal to whatever holds its interest. In addition, it is full of confidence in the future, being competitive, ambitious, assertive and (on the negative side) improvident. The Sun in a fire sign craves freedom and opportunities for self-improvement but, most of all, needs a steady stream of opportunities. It does not have to use them as long as it knows they are there to use. The Sun in fire hates routine but welcomes adventure, no matter whether the latter is of the physical or of the mental variety. Such restlessness means that the native is not very particular about forms: whether they are physical or abstract, he finds it hard to know what to do with them. Yet there is a "plus"; because he intuitively gets behind mere forms, and searches into the origins, the development and the inner connection of things, he is therefore in a position to integrate the various components of his psyche.

Because it represents the combination of the cardinal cross with the element fire, Aries is the most outgoing of the three fire signs: its natives have the most need to be up and doing, even though sometimes they get no more done in the end. Both the element fire, with its flare for self-advertisement, and the cardinal cross, with its assimilation processes, are oriented toward the outside world; which means that Aries subjects have to live restless, adventurous lives with plenty of possibilities in order to maintain their equilibrium and in order to respond to their many inner drives. The various factors in their psyches are best integrated in this way, even though others may find their continual changes of direction baffling.

When able to develop his full potential, the Aries subject comes over as energetic, warm, buoyant and enthusiastic. As a cardinal cross-fire combination, this individual will quickly take the initiative, but will not always see things through. Aries derives self-confidence from pioneering and from the independence with which

Aries goes his own way. Involved in the outside world (cardinal cross) and yet turned inward (fire element), Aries can indulge in competitive pursuits (sports for example), while feeding a sense of self-importance at the same time. Hence Aries is often ready for a fight, but only while he can maintain an interest in the cause of the moment; for Aries does need change (fire), especially in the outside world (cardinal cross). And this individual so moves into the world both literally and figuratively (in contrast, for example, to someone under Cancer who, although also a member of the cardinal cross, works with a much more inward-looking element).

If the Arian energy has no proper channels of expression, it will break out turbulently; instead of healthy competition, the subject goes in for outright aggression even to the point of violence. Aries has no respect for the feelings of others. And, even in the most extreme fits of egotism, membership in the cardinal cross does mean that Aries needs an environment to respond to (or shall we say to kick at?). For this reason, Aries is sometimes regarded as the most unfeeling of the signs, one that wants to walk over everybody. That, however, is a very simplistic view of the sign. Any trouble may be traced to an overspilling of dammed energy; and then Aries is put down as blind and impulsive because it is hard to say where the next breach in the dam will occur.

The great vitality of the Aries type makes for courage, and these natives will devote themselves with considerable fervor to "fiery" ideals and aims. The picture suggested by the combination of the element fire and the cardinal cross is of people who are happiest when rushing on the world, conquering it and experiencing it intensely—in spite of the fact that fire is so strongly rooted in itself. The energy of Aries *will* out, restrictions or no restrictions, rules or no rules.

MOON IN ARIES

The unconscious emotional response to the environment typical of the element fire combined with the cardinal cross is the resultant of two outgoing tendencies, one belonging to behavior (fire), the other belonging to the mode of assimilation (cardinal cross). But the individual with the Moon in Aries is not equipped to storm the world so impetuously as the individual with the Sun in Aries.

Someone with Moon in Aries sallies forth because it feels good or because the situation is insecure. The Aries Moon is ever on the watch for fresh stimuli in surroundings and eagerly seizes on those things which can be identified emotionally. Feelings are soon stirred, but enthusiasm for what stirs them cools just as quickly. This is all of a piece with the need for plenty of change and adventure. The Aries Moon will devote a great deal of energy (fire) to things which (usually temporarily) are attractive, and will impatiently brush aside anything that frustrates this need. The emotional structure of Moon in Aries makes the nature very ready to enter the fray, if not to provoke it in the first place. Owing to an emotional identification with things, this Moon sign is not afraid to let it be known that it stands for this, then for that and then for the other; and so the Aries Moon appears to be full of self-confidence. Freedom is very dear, which makes this individual particularly sensitive to any restraints (because the cardinal cross likes to take the initiative and fire is egocentric). This person can quickly feel and act like a cornered animal.

The directness and impulsiveness of fire means that in difficult situations people with the Moon in Aries soon become irritated, speak sharply and lose their temper quite easily—more easily in fact than people with Sun in Aries. And when everything is going swimmingly, they are quickly carried away by fresh currents. Those with Moon in Aries are happiest in a free, independent and changeable position, whether in business life or in social situations. The person with Moon in Aries prefers activities which are subject to as few restrictions as possible and can look to the future full of enthusiasm. We say "look to" the future advisedly, since actually planning for the future is not in the nature.

Subjects with Moon in Aries have such strong self-motivation arising from the unconscious mind that they do not always take the wishes of others into account. They do not intend to be hurtful, but can be so carried away by the cause of the moment that they think of nothing else. They do not hide their light under a bushel, and are often accused of being pushy and publicity seeking. But this is not their purpose. It need hardly be said that home life makes up only a small part of their world, and Moon in Aries is said to make a person undomesticated and unfeeling. The part about being undomesticated may be true, but it is too much of an oversimplification to say they are unfeeling; the so-called insensitivity is part and parcel of the need to get out in the world regardless of home ties. To prevent them from living this sort of life will only make them "cool off." The world is their home and that is where they want to be. The Moon in Aries makes people more sensitive in this respect than does the Sun, because the Moon has an unconscious need to feel comfortable. Therefore the reactions of the Moon in Aries can be fiercer and more violent than those of the Sun in Aries.

MERCURY IN ARIES

Just as with the Sun and Moon, this position gives a very outward-looking impulse. Mercury in Aries symbolizes quick and smooth contacts which are often frank and open-hearted (fire). The native does not look for any depth in these contacts, but values them for their number and variety, and also for the progress they help him to make. Mercury in Aries handles its mental activities by getting heavily involved in the external world (cardinal cross!), and the native's attention is absorbed in what is going on around him.

The liveliness of the element fire, stimulated still further by the cardinal cross, makes the thinking of Mercury in Aries quick; it is short, sharp, resolute. Owing to the strong ego-involvement of fire, Mercury in Aries does not shrink from sticking to an opinion; what is more, Aries being a cardinal sign, this opinion is voiced openly. The way in which the subject assimilates ideas is by confronting them with the outside world. That fierce arguments can arise from this is pretty obvious. Because of the tendency to individuality and originality of Mercury in Aries, the subject likes to be provocative in thought and in expression, and will defend the opposite point of view "just for the fun of it." The love of freedom typical of Mercury in fire signs manifests here in thinking and communication in a cardinal manner. This placement needs plenty of scope in the outside world for the free expression of personal opinion, independence and freedom; otherwise the individual is unable to let people know how he is reacting—with all the consequences of that restriction.

As a planet, Mercury represents the way in which we try to make sense of our world; it represents our mental activity. Mercury in Aries displays great mental activity, but this is not to say that everyone with Mercury in that position is a mental giant. What is true is that the brain of an individual with Mercury in Aries is always busy: thoughts are never still. Therefore he is liable to be tense and overexcited, and this can show itself in one of several different ways, such as incessant chattering, inability to stop and listen to others, insomnia, jumping to conclusions and lack of concentration. On the credit side, Mercury in Aries is ideal for making quick decisions, for quick mental reactions and for a fluent and flashing style of speech.

Mercury in fire makes for someone who dares to stand up for what he or she believes, and with the cardinal cross, that person's ideas are immediately put into words. With Mercury in Aries fresh thoughts and inspirations follow one another in such quick succession that the subject has no chance to think twice about anything. Obviously, this makes for new and highly original points of view, even though they are not always practical or realistic.

VENUS IN ARIES

Venus in Aries is ardent and enthusiastic in its way of rushing into emotional contacts. The fire-cardinal cross combination gives a strongly outward-looking desire for comfort and safety. The individual with Venus in Aries will therefore experience a need for warm and passionate friendships and romantic affairs which are adventurous, smooth-running and full of variety. To tell the truth, Venus is more impulsive here than anywhere else in the zodiac.

The element fire makes the love instinct rather idealistic. That is to say, Venus in Aries needs a relationship that is not based on material security, but on some ideal, even though an innate restlessness means that the ideal is liable to change. The freedom demanded by fire also plays an important part in the expression of the feelings because, although fire will eagerly enter into a love relationship, it wants to preserve its independence. Hence Venus in Aries may favor light attachments, free love, open marriages and, in general, relationships that allow both partners to go their own way most of the time. Fire, with its need to dart here and there, wants room to maneuver within the emotional bond. This may mean that, in addition to a main commitment, the person with Venus in Aries (fire plus the outward-looking cardinal cross) also wants to keep options open for the enjoyment of other relationships, regardless of their type or duration. However, this is not a hard-and-fast rule. If the other partner continues to fascinate and knows how to inject enough variety into life, the need for new impulses and possibilities can be satisfied within the existing union. Venus in Aries does not bestow any special penchant for adultery (as some books would have us believe!); nevertheless, the capacity for giving and receiving love and for appreciating beauty is so high-powered in Aries that often the narrow family circle is felt to be too limited or too limiting.

The need for beauty, which Venus expresses as a psychic factor, is not always, in the fire sign Aries, in harmony with the prevailing norms and standards. External form, or form as such, does little for Venus in Aries. Venus here tries to discern the idea behind the form, and the inner connection of that idea with other ideas or possibilities. *This* is what Venus in Aries experiences as beauty and concord.

Venus in Aries has a great deal of warmth to shed on surroundings, and is what one tends to think of as a typical Venus. Because Aries involves itself, sometimes all too willingly, in its surroundings, Venus here can impress one with the wonderful warmth and sincerity of her feelings. However, while sensitivity is not lacking, there is also an element of bluntness. Once the blaze of passion has died down, the Aries Venus can ditch the loved one without ceremony in order to captivate someone else with those fiery charms; there is no deliberate intention to wound, just a hankering for change and for something new. This behavior may easily cause people to say that Venus in Aries is hard and unfeeling; but if the other party severs the relationship, this Venus can feel it deeply. The fact is this: Aries uses the world as a workshop for hammering out problems and difficulties, and a new conquest appeals to it as a very good way of solving an old problem.

MARS IN ARIES

Mars in Aries is in its own sign. Here it is free to develop all its qualities (both "good" and "bad") to their fullest extent. Power and energy are intensified by a fire sign, and in a cardinal sign the activities are aimed straight at the environment. Hence it is not surprising that Mars in Aries gives the impression of being too energetic or dynamic.

Mars is that force in people that tends to set us apart from the group. Aries, being both energetic and outgoing, bestows on Mars a great capability for action. And so the egocentricity of Mars plus the egocentricity of this fire sign gives people with Mars in Aries a strong desire to go their own way and "hang the consequences." The energy available is formidable (energy in a fire sign!), so we can expect these people with Mars in Aries to have great powers of endurance.

When people with an Arian Mars are interested in something, they can devote themselves to it one hundred per cent, certain that the fiery vision within will work out in practice. Mars in Aries indicates a courage and self-confidence that can border on recklessness, or insist on one's point of view, and if necessary, the ability to fight for it (either physically or mentally). The obvious danger is the egotism that comes from relying too much on one's own reasoning. Should circumstances manage to block the martian energy, the pent-up feelings will discharge themselves, sooner or later, in aggressiveness, unpredictability, irresponsibility, and even in acts of violence.

This placement of Mars favors activities requiring prompt action, comptetiveness, vigor and initiative; it also favors pioneering and work calling for the application of brute strength. Initiative and the desire to break fresh ground have their destructive side but can indirectly lead to renewal where the existing state of affairs is forcibly destroyed for replacement by something new. Mars in Aries may make the native appear course and uncultured, since social graces mean little or nothing to this combination; nevertheless, the native is often the proverbial "rough diamond."

The Arian Mars presents the picture of one who is an energetic self-starter, ardent, combative, brave and independent; also one addicted to change, new things and adventure. The surplus energy, which is not so easy to channel in present-day society, can manifest as short-lived belligerence until a fresh distraction comes along. For Mars in Aries, tension is best relieved by engaging in strenuous physical or mental activity. Sitting still doing nothing or being tied to routine work can be very destructive.

JUPITER IN ARIES

The urge to expand, typical of Jupiter, is particularly strong when the planet is in Aries. Jupiter always indicates a widening of the horizons, and the element fire likes nothing better. The planet is ever on the watch for new possibilities, and the cardinal cross brings this characteristic into the open. Therefore, when Jupiter is in Aries we can speak of the need for a changing spectrum of experiences and an increasing range of vision; also for the need to give bold and (above all) individualistic expression to the urge for expansion and inner growth. A supply of new ideas is required to feed this inner growth. The need for spiritual and religious experience generates the need for many and varied impressions coming in from the outside world; but a Jupiter in Aries can also project its own ardent convictions back onto the outside world with great enthusiasm.

The desire for outward expansion means that the person with Jupiter in Aries wants to enjoy an adventurous and carefree life, with something new and exciting always in prospect. However, not enough time is taken in exploring each experience in depth—the urge to move on is too imperative.

Freedom and the opportunity to develop have almost religious overtones for those with Jupiter in Aries, and they will devote themselves to aims which have these ideals in view. The aims need not be self-centered; they can also be related to everything going on in the outside world. The cardinal cross, as we already know, directs any energy available to it into the outside world.

Although, owing to the fact that Aries is a fire sign, Jupiter expresses itself in that sign with a certain amount of egotism, its expansiveness is nevertheless willingly used on behalf of the environment. The native is able to lend enthusiastic aid to building up whatever is helpful to the community. The satisfaction this brings and the appreciation shown by others go to help the inner growth of the individual.

SATURN IN ARIES

The introverted, uncommunicative behavior typical of Saturn can scarcely find expression in Aries, the most extraverted of the zodiacal signs. Saturn-consciousness forms slowly and is strongly individualistic, but Aries does not give enough time for its development.

The sense of responsibility of Saturn accords ill with such an adventurous and change-seeking sign as Aries. Hence we find the native either acting thoughtlessly and irresponsibly, or else getting himself well and truly entrenched in matters with which he identifies, regardless of whether his projects are viable or not. The carefree, adventurous kind of life symbolized by Aries is hard for someone to reconcile with the urge to lay down exact boundaries, and he can seek to deal with the problem in one of two ways: either he avoids confrontations and suffers from an anxiety neurosis characterized by the fear of not being a success in life, or else he overcompensates the anxiety with spasmodic demonstrations of how adventurous he really is. It need hardly be said that this frame of mind can lead to irresponsible actions. A lack of self-confidence is also to blame for this.

Saturn, as the "learning process through pain" will, when in Aries, throw the individual back on himself through his own ill-considered actions and the difficulties which arise from them. If he learns from this, he will gain the strength to develop his own unique character. But the road is usually hard and long because it is so difficult for Saturn to unfold its potential in Aries.

URANUS, NEPTUNE AND PLUTO IN ARIES

A certain amount of heed has to be paid to the collective factor in our interpretation of the planets Jupiter and Saturn (see Chapter Two), and now, as we come to consider the planets Uranus, Neptune and Pluto, we find that this factor has taken over completely.[18] Whole generations of people have these planets in the same signs, and although they do express themselves in keeping with the nature of the sign, we must beware of attaching any direct personal significance to them. Generally speaking, we can say that the inner compulsion to break molds and the need for originality (Uranus), the need to refine and to transcend form—or to reduce it to chaos (Neptune), and the need for power, confrontation and transcendence of form (Pluto), will, when these planets are in Aries, impinge in a very direct and uninhibited manner on the outside world. The energies in question contain a certain amount of (unconscious) egoism and accomplish their work out of things which are immaterial. Their task is made easier by confrontations in the outer world (cardinal cross!).

Folks with Uranus in Aries will clearly have the need to try and develop their own potential and to demand liberty. Personal freedom is very important to them. It is remarkable that, during the transit of Uranus through this sign, depth psychology (psychoanalysis) broke fresh ground. Even today we can still take advantage of this in order to learn to develop and to express our personalities to better advantage, and to "become someone." As the first sign of the zodiac, Aries invariably seems to represent the first stage in a new cycle, when the old is sealed off and the new is ready to begin. Thus Uranus in Aries represents the means and opportunities for developing the individuality in alternative ways, and people who have this placement will share these features of their birth era and will want to "do their own thing" as the saying goes.

Neptune in Aries has a somewhat different effect. Personal identity and the development of individual potential fade into the background. But they assume finer forms for the benefit of that individual who is mature enough to handle the subtle vibrations of Neptune.

It remains to be seen how Pluto (and Neptune, too, for that matter) will fully express its influence in this sign; but we may surely expect new individual developments and the start of some significant advances—as well as power struggles and personal confrontations. Yet, whatever the case, it is true of all the planets that, when in this sign, they make themselves felt in the outside world and develop and express their potential in it. Whether consciously or unconsciously, thier influences and their confrontations are best assimilated in a cardinal cross situation when projected into the outside world.

2. FIXED FIRE: LEO

SUN IN LEO

The characteristics of the Sun in the element fire are again found in the sign of Leo, but the way in which the Leo subject assimilates experiences is in total contrast to the way in which experiences are assimilated by the Aries subject. Whereas in Aries everything turns to the outer world and experiences an interaction with it, in Leo attention is paid mainly to the inner world and to the personal inner voice. In Leo, that is to say, the conscious mind focuses on the internal desires of the psyche issuing from the unconscious. If those with Leo Sun signs are able to develop naturally, then unlike Aries natives, they work out the implications and problems of everyday life within themselves. The external world, which has given rise to these implications and problems, plays no further active part in this process. Aries subjects respond with bursts of fierce activity, while Leo subjects engage in activity which, though hidden, is just as intense.

Listening to the inner voice is, in the fixed cross, not so much a matter of conscious intent as it is something taken for granted. In fact, it is hard for someone belonging to one of the fixed signs to comprehend any other way of proceeding. Although folks belonging to the cardinal and mutable signs do share the characteristics to a lesser extent, it is typical of the fixed cross because in the fixed cross everything emanates from the self.

To put it rather picturesquely, we may say that fire strikes inward in order to consume the mental fuel constantly being piled up by the activities of the fixed cross. So the individual with the Sun in Leo will try to come to terms with himself directly, and not via the outside world—hence the accusation of extreme egotism often leveled at Leo subjects, an accusation that has some degree of truth in it, since it goes without saying that when the self-interest of the fire element is combined with the self-rootedness of the fixed cross little room is left for thinking of others. But this does not mean that the Leo subject will go through life as a lonely egotist; quite the reverse. Leo can do much for others for the very reason that he is so much involved with himself. The strength lies in the battle with the unconscious; if Leo can hold his own there, self-development will be much helped and self-confidence will be strengthened. And the Leo who radiates this strong self-confidence can prove an encouragement to those in the immediate environment.

All the same, the battle with the unconscious can give Leos a fixation on certain things, *or* on the conflict itself (the crisis), *or* on avoiding the conflict. In the latter attempt they will not be successful, because the fixed cross is part of their "standard equipment" which will continually confront them with their own unconscious. People with the Sun in Leo can become, owing to the presence of the fixed cross in their Sun sign, inspiring leaders or veritable despots according to which side of the character comes out on top.

Because the fixed cross in the sign Leo is continually dredging up unconscious factors into the light of day, the ego (symbolized by the Sun) is everlastingly being confronted with the "primeval ocean" from which it is attempting to distance itself in the slow trek to maturity. As we have seen, the element and cross combined in Leo both emphasize the ego, so this process is very unsettling. Therefore the Leo native has a craving for recognition and for occupying a position of authority, power and the like. And it is true enough that out of these struggles with personal uncertainty come qualities such as leadership, willpower, self-confidence and dignity; but if hindrances and blockages come into play, the warmth of Leo can vanish in egocentricity, self-interest, imperiousness, tyranny on some scale or other, ostentation, boasting, displays of strength and so on.

The lust for living typical of fire is also present in Leo, but is much more banked up inside than in the other fire signs. Leo subjects can dispense with wide-ranging adventures and will remain content with confinement to a single place and with concentration on a single issue, just so long as these are of use to them in the fight against inner insecurity.

This internal struggle (of which Leo does not need to be conscious—it is something completely natural to the sign!) is also the reason why we read in some astrology books that if you give enough praise and a sufficient number of pats on the back Leo will keep on trying to please you. For Leo finds all appreciation supportive, whether it be sincere or insincere. But when we go on to read in the same astrological literature about Leo's superb self-confidence, we have to remember that this sign is not self-confident through and through; Leo merely behaves in a self-confident manner because that is the most suitable way to develop in keeping with inner desires. There is a weak spot that Leo is trying to make good. By acting confidently this sign instinctively senses he will acquire genuine self-confidence. Nevertheless, self-confidence is a problem, and this is the basis of the often heard remark that an offended Leo will drop you like the proverbial hot potato. By hurting Leo's self-esteem you make him feel restrained, and this is something he cannot stand (either consciously or unconsciously): his energy *must* break through. The touchiness and the all-too quickly aroused aggression, also the accumulation of status symbols such as diplomas, medals and other palpable evidences of recognition, can all be explained in terms of the fixed cross. The fixed cross brings to the surface traces of its inferior element buried in the unconscious: in this case, the element earth. Earth is decidedly concrete and concerned with the physical appearance of things. Leo's weak spot is therefore to be found in a confrontation with the physical (which Leo feels compelled to integrate with the personality), and in insecurity (another consequence of the activity of the fixed cross). Hence there is nothing strange in Leo taking an overdose of material things (putting on a show of luxury) in order to dull a sense of insecurity.

At the same time, the element earth is not one of the main constituents of the conscious mind in Leo, quite the contrary. Therefore Leo's treatment of material wealth is very uncertain. At one moment Leo must own everything, and the following moment Leo will happily give it all away. Gifts in kind (often made with regal bounty) may even be used to create self-confidence and to win praise. In this sense, the fixed cross offers Leo the opportunity to employ the contents of the unconscious in an unconscious manner in order to keep the conscious mind more firmly in the saddle.

To sum up, Leo is full of dynamism, vitality, warmth and creativity, but all are very inward-looking. The confrontatin thus brought about with the unconscious makes Leo unsure of self, and this is an aspect of personality that Leo does best to overcome in order to achieve full maturity. Loyalty, generosity, the exercise of willpower, and ambition, can assist in this task. But, if frustrated, there can be a fairly quick degeneration into egocentricity, power-seeking and so on. All these forms of expression, however inconsistent and conflicting they may appear, spring from the selfsame source: the combination of a fiery attitude to life with a fixed (regressive) mode of assimilating life's experiences.

MOON IN LEO

Here the Moon is positioned where the outgoing element fire is held in check by the fixed cross: the energy of fire is drained into the psyche and little of its animation and enthusiasm escapes into the environment. Because of the regressive nature of the energy flow, unconscious factors regularly erupt into the field of consciousness, creating feelings of insecurity—as we have already seen when considering the Sun in Leo. However, with Moon in Leo, the results are somewhat different, for the Moon has more need than the Sun has for security and, when threatened with insecurity, it is quicker to overcompensate.

People with the Moon in Leo need to know they are fulfilling a definite function in the immediate neighborhood and in society as a whole. This is not due, as it was with the cardinal cross, to any close involvement with the whole, but is due to feelings of personal insecurity evoked in the conscious mind by various currents of influence welling up from the unconscious. Overcompensation usually takes the form of bumptiousness. Because the fixed cross in this sign erodes confidence, the Moon will encourage overcompensation more readily when in Leo than when in any other sign, and we are justified in saying that people with a Leo Moon will have a distinct need to exercise authority and to receive honor and recognition both at home and in society. This can make the tyrant, but, on the other hand, it can produce people who are so grateful to those who show them respect that they will shower others with tokens of friendship. Therefore they can do well as community leaders, even though they may not tolerate much in the way of criticism (others must not find out how unsure of themselves they really are!). Moon in Leo can also make good and fair-minded family men—except that they will not suffer their wives and children to question decisions.

The need for change is still present, but is not of decisive importance. In this connection, the fixed cross tends to bring to the surface the element fire's opposite number, earth; when the Moon in in Leo, this can happen so as to increase the need for comfort and safety at the most unexpected moments, especially on the purely physical plane. Therefore (in contrast to what occurs when the Moon is in the other fire signs) the Moon in Leo does not incline people to be overeager to leave their places for the sake of taking a look at new possibilities. Rather, they do their best to settle down where they are so long as they can win respect and honor there.

With this birth chart position, personal worth and personal freedom are both very important. One should avoid offending those with Moon in Leo; they are so sensitive. On the other hand they like compliments and, owing to the naiveté of fire and the vanity arising from insecurity, they often fall for flattery.

However, if those who have Moon in Leo are given the chance to be magnanimous and to feel valued by the community, we can bask in all the warmth they have to bestow.

MERCURY IN LEO

The facts encountered by Mercury in Leo subjects on the path through life are assimilated in an idealistic (fire-type) manner and they will try to discover their possibilities and developments (i.e., their inner connection with other facts). There is a strong desire to look behind physical appearances and to trace the broad outlines; however, since the fixed cross mentality is so busily engaged internally, Mercury in Leo is not so quick to say what it thinks. This Mercury will hold its peace if necessary, but that does not mean that the natives keep silent inside. They think things through—much further, in fact, than the concrete situation of the moment. Fire tends to expand its horizons, and when Mercury is in fire signs the thinking itself is expansive to the extent that the thinker finds small details unimportant and concentrates on the larger issues.

People with Mercury in Leo immerse themselves—both literally and metaphorically—in whatever engages their attention (fixed cross!). They do not work quickly, and most of what is done originates from within. Vision can be great, and yet it usually bears the stamp of personality, since fire is always consumed with self and the fixed cross mainly listens to the demands of the inner life. What is more, the fixed cross is responsible for the surfacing of the contents of the unconscious, which, with Mercury in Leo, has the consequences not only of allowing the element earth that is buried in the unconscious to play some part in the thinking (yet only involuntarily, as we see in Chapter Seven for example), but also of imparting to the thinking certain tendencies which undermine the ego. This means that with Mercury in Leo, much more than with the other fire signs, there is a certain materialistic cast of mind, and that, owing to a sense of uncertainty underlying the thinking, Mercury will try to compensate by seeking recognition and praise for analysis and planning. If recognition and praise are not given, Mercury will brook no contradiction but will go on to conceive increasingly grandiose ideas until gradually losing touch with reality. But if the person with Mercury in Leo is accorded the honor he thinks he deserves, and if we are prepared to trust him, Mercury here will pay us with a proud but very warm helpfulness.

This planet provides us with information about an individual's manner of communicating, and Mercury in Leo inclines one to a somewhat authoritative way of speaking. Self-conscious expression and the use of language to enhance status are a feature. The approach to contacts and conversations is affable and genuine; but if crossed, the native will indulge in boastfulness and swank. The thinking and communicating of someone with Mercury in Leo is strongly colored by the personality, since insecurity makes one long to be important.

VENUS IN LEO

The desire for harmony and beauty, for warmth and love, is expressed here in a Leo-like way: it is fiery, intense, vivacious and egocentric (fire); however, the fixed cross influence restrains the impetuosity of fire. Venus in Leo is much affected by whatever rises from the unconscious via the fixed cross. The contents surface involuntarily every now and again, and have to be heeded if a feeling of well-being is to be preserved. The Venusian longing for harmony, beauty and love expressed through fiery Leo is often mingled with unconscious earth characteristics, namely the need for material security. A hankering after the good things in life is typical of Venus in Leo. But the activity of the submerged earth element is unpredictable and can show itself on occasion as the impulse to give possessions away or to gamble them away—by which, incidentally, fire will seek to open up future options.

The undermining effect of the fixed cross is very marked with Venus in this position: it feeds the sense of insecurity. The person with Venus in Leo needs—and demands—plenty of attention and reassurance. If a woman with this placement in her horoscope has a sense of frustration and insecurity, she will make her husband wait on her hand and foot, and constantly minister to her desires. He will have to go on presenting his offerings to her in an attitude of adoration, and in return will be kept self-effacing and docile by her wifely disciplining—because she will insist that he does exactly what he is told without argument or discussion once her mind is made up.

In the ordinary way, however, the wife with Venus in this position blossoms as the old-fashioned good hostess. The appreciation this brings to the Venus in Leo fortifies her ego. The gentle side of Venus in the "royal" sign Leo often makes for a charming personality, and as a lover she can be extremely passionate, even though this does not always appear on the surface in the first instance. Preserving her own dignity, which is so important in personally vulnerable Leo, plays a definite part here. Any frustrations in this area can lead to ostentatious displays of her own importance, and she will use her womanliness as a means to dominate people and situations. That she can throw money around like royal bounty on occasion goes without saying.

On the other hand, Venus in Leo can extend warm and willing help to anyone who suffers an injustice. Venus in this sign is only too ready to lend assistance to restore the balance in such cases, but in such a way as to feed the native's sense of self-importance.

MARS IN LEO

Mars in fire signs invariably places a great deal of energy at the disposal of the native. So Mars in Leo can be very lively and energetic, but here also what is done springs from a need to strengthen the ego. Mars in Leo can do mighty deeds and can plow through a great deal of work, but the native does expect recognition for it. Because the fixed cross constantly confronts him with his insecurity, he craves to be acknowledged in every possible way in the world at large. If recognition is withheld from him in his own field of operations, this can lead to outright aggression. On the other hand, given adequate support and well-deserved compliments, he will work with indefatigable energy. But the praise must be well earned, as fire is very upright in these matters; only if he suffers great obstructions will the person with Mars in Leo claim more honor than is due.

The need for honor and for recognition of ability makes someone with Mars in Leo too proud to turn out poor workmanship. Competitiveness incites this individual to work well because Mars here wants to be the best, the quickest and so on.

Aggression and fierce responses are all too quickly unleashed with Mars in Leo when the individuality is under attack. Self-affirmation is a characteristic common to Mars and to the sign Leo (fire element and fixed cross). Therefore people with Mars in Leo have a strong need for personal identity, for a recognizable and valued ego. Although appreciation is sought in the outside world, it is only by way of confirmation of their own assessment of their worth. In this connection, the inner voice is what is most important for the fixed cross, and the search for recognition in the outside world must not be confused with activities of the fixed cross; rather it is caused by the need of the conscious mind to oppose the unconscious mind. It is by listening to the inner voice that people with Mars in Leo can assimilate personal patterns of activity. Irritation is not so much directed against the recipient of their outbursts as against the inner struggle to find adequate expression of their individuality. It is entirely possible that those with Mars in Leo will make capable leaders; the reverse side of the coin is that they will get others to do the dirty work. However, the nub of the matter is that Mars in Leo will look for self-satisfaction by competitiveness, activity and hard work.

JUPITER IN LEO

The expansive psychic contents symbolized by the planet Jupiter are not easy to involve in details when this planet is in Leo. The fire of Leo will make itself felt in the long run. Broad outlines and new developments are what interest fire, not the minutiae. Jupiter fully concurs in this, so that, with this placement, we can speak of plenty of willing, of making ambitious plans and of a strong orientation toward expansion, and so on. But also the insecure ego of the apparently so self-assured Leo who seems to court attention will play an important part in the way in which Jupiter expresses itself. Jupiter will try to compensate (or overcompensate) this insecurity by coming on stage full of jovial grandeur. Jupiter in Leo can make one preeminently regal and dignified; but the unconscious contents of the element earth, which surface via the fixed cross, can also give Jupiter in Leo the desire to strut about in finery and to show off possessions.

Equally prominent is the religious and spiritual side of Jupiter in Leo. There is a feeling for deeper values, regardless of how these relate to everyday living. An important social position in which people with Jupiter in Leo can do as much good as they are able is one possibility. They may also take up religious work: the warmth and joviality of Jupiter in the element fire can encourage others with its enthusiasm. The activity of the fixed cross gives the outside world the impression that the warmth of Jupiter in Leo comes from within.

For Jupiter, as for other planets in Leo, appreciation is important. If this is gained, the individual will be goodness itself; but if Leo has to fight for recognition, extremely personal and egotistic motives can come into play and the native can become involved in all kinds of power struggles and conflicts with authority.

SATURN IN LEO

Leo is a difficult position for Saturn. To begin with, the element fire is not an ideal setting for this influence because the extravert and forward-looking character of that element ill accords with an introverted impulse that is chiefly concerned with what happens in the here and now. The presence of the fixed cross might make it appear that Saturn will be to some extent at home in this sign, but that is a mistake. Saturn, as the principle that enables people to build up consciousness, is invariably confronted in Leo with all kinds of influences arising from the unconscious which undermine conscious life by their very uncertainty—thus giving Leo such a strong need for reassurance. And so this consciousness-building force of Saturn has a double fight on its hands. On the one hand, this inward-looking force has to try and hold its own in an outgoing sign, and, on the other hand, it must counteract the constant flow of disruptive uncertainties coming from within. Saturn in Leo can react like a cornered animal to any interference from outside. The ego is more sensitive here than it is anywhere else, and so there is a sort of permanent authority crisis.

None of this means that people with Saturn in Leo are doomed to go through life depressed and discontented. In fact, they may live fairly cheerfully, even though the presence of Saturn will temper somewhat the brightness of fire. Others would do well to remember that people with this placement are so sensitive on the subject of ego-identity and of developing personal awareness that they will tolerate little or no comment on it. It is a consciousness of their need in this direction that makes them so touchy.

As with all the placements of Saturn, here also there are two possible reactions. Either we see someone who overcompensates with Leo-like qualities—an irresponsible hedonist who hides a lack of an ego-identity behind a luxurious life-style—or we see someone who approaches life's pleasures with nervous anxiety, diffidence and feelings of guilt. Both forms of behavior can, of course, alternate in the same individual. The most significant feature of Saturn in Leo is that the need to establish a stable self-awareness is not only very great, it is also the tenderest spot in the psyche.

URANUS, NEPTUNE AND PLUTO IN LEO

The collective character of these planets makes personal interpretation difficult. Generally speaking, we can say that the tendency to break the mold of form and the urge to be original (Uranus), the desire to refine form, to dissolve its outlines and to make it universal (Neptune), and the need for power, confrontation and the transcendence of form (Pluto), will, when these planets are in Leo, be expressed in a fiery (or ardent) way, yet, because of the involvement of the fixed cross, not with extreme vehemence. Due to the fire element they psychic energies will to some extent be ego-oriented; also a considerable amount of unconscious material will be given expression (fixed cross). Inner confrontations are highly likely. Take Pluto in Leo for example. This placement is to be found in the horoscopes of people now between 27 and 45 years old. These people seem to be irresistibly drawn into power struggles with other age groups. Because the Plutonic influence is trying to escape from the cells of the unconscious mind, freedom for self-expression may become an absolute necessity, especially during the years of growing up.

Uranus in Leo has the urge to express its identity in highly original and unusual ways. When taken to extremes, this urge can lead to intolerance which can even menace the identity of others.

The generation with Neptune in Leo lived through an era of unprecedented expansion (from the First World War to the threshold of the 1930s), but has had to pay for its great expectations with a chaotic, worldwide identity crisis. Neptune entered Leo ahead of Pluto and Uranus and broke up the settled soil of the ego of mankind, readying it for the transforming and renewing work of the latter planets in subsequent decades.

3. MUTABLE FIRE: SAGITTARIUS

SUN IN SAGITTARIUS

The third fire sign has inherited the mutable cross as part of its equipment, which means that it is neither completely orientated toward the external world (as the cardinal cross is) nor completely governed by the inner voice (as the fixed cross is). Its strength lies in the ability to switch from one mode to the other, so that a Sagittarian at his best learns to combine opposites and has the possibility of achieving a warm and lively wisdom. At its worst, Sagittarius is colorless and without a sense of direction, even though the fieriness in the nature can still blaze out on occasion.

Although, as a member of one of the fire signs, Sagittarians may be characterized as outgoing, the mutable cross influence does exert an inward pull in spite of its unmistakable liking for manifestation. A regressive energy flow confronts these natives with the contents of their unconscious in such a way that for a while they may become as self-absorbed as a Leo; and yet, being mutable, they will bounce back into society full of fire and verve as if nothing had happened. To the world at large this looks like capriciousness, but Sagittarians need plenty of change. They seek many and varied experiences in order to integrate them in a fire-sign way. They want to trace the thin red skein running through the fabric of life, and they use their intuition to find hidden connections. Being in a position to see possibilities is essential to the peace of mind of Sagittarians, owing to their ardor combined with a liking for change. It is this that gives them such optimism. The object of their search hardly matters if it has the virtue of being new and somehow ties in with the way they are going: the hope is that it will bring fresh options into either inner or outer life. This is the sign that likes to widen its horizons. If this can be achieved, the natives feel that things are "moving" and are content with all the fresh impulses with which they are occupied. Their mutability is then held in balance. But if unable to explore or to keep active (either physically or mentally), they cannot be themselves and are much less favorably placed to solve problems.

Impelled by restlessness, by enthusiasm and by a desire to press forward into the future, they set themselves high ideals. However, these may be impossible of attainment in spite of the best endeavors; also, since these ideas are seldom down to earth they may have little immediate value.

Mutability can prove a danger to Sagittarians when their search for fresh stimuli and new things can become so feverish that they lose touch with everyday reality. The (intuitive) making and breaking of connections can become nothing more than a habit.

Because the mutable cross influence allows the release of unconscious factors from time to time, the life of the mind is another area which may appeal to the Sagittarian as suitable for exploration. Out of the inner life this sign can crystallize standards that will faithfully be kept, and they may well become known for great knowledge of recondite matters. In other words, natives of this sign who are well endowed intellectually may become theoretical scientists or metaphysicians, bent on exploring the boundaries of understanding. If the flow of psychic energy is impeded, it will pile up behind the blockage and then break through into over-compensation. The mutable cross is split between cardinal cross (outer world) and fixed cross (inner world) characteristics; and so the internal life inevitably runs into the outer life—making the natives appear somewhat egocentric to peers: they attach more importance to personal opinions that to those of others. They will listen to what someone else has to say, but will then try to put him right or at least to manage him so that he cannot take his independent line.

The fire-mutability combination means that Sagittarians have a need for everything new and full of potential. They can rush at things like an Aries and yet have the internal preoccupations of Leo—hence ambition is one of the likely characteristics of Sagit-tarius. However, fire alone is not enough. Take away the chance to connect one thing to another, to institute changes, to integrate and, in short, to work toward a synthesis, and Sagittarius will be utterly miserable and will find it hard to make contact with the inner self.

MOON IN SAGITTARIUS

When the Moon is in Sagittarius, it can give open expression to the animated and fiery qualities of the element in which it stands due to the partly outward flow of psychic energy. Just as with Sun in Sagittarius, the mutability is very pronounced. Because the mutable cross works both inwardly and outwardly, we find that the behavior of those with Moon in Sagittarius will waver in situations which are emotional or emotionally insecure, between withdrawal to listen to an inner voice and, on the other hand, reactions betraying dependence on the environment and the outside world. Sometimes there can be such changes in demeanor that the world will experience difficulty in understanding them. Since the mutable cross influence will draw out energy from the unconscious from time to time (something that the fixed cross does continually), those with Moon in Sagittarius can feel insecure in this area of the emotions and may not know quite how to react. These confronta-tions with the inner and outer worlds make the Moon in Sagittarius person a seeker; the cross in which the Moon is placed gives changeableness and a need for new things. The element brings variety and alternation. In such conditions, there is a craving for anything that will expand the horizons either physically or mentally. So that here, too, we can have the philosopher, the explorer of spiritual or inner values.

Moon-sign Sagittarians are not comfortable unless they are free to turn their minds to higher things and to develop potential for the spiritual and for the mind-expanding. And they will not leave the outside world in ignorance of this. In uncertain situations they are soon on their feet trying to lead the conversation in this direction, eagerly letting others know something of their own insights and endeavoring to make others share their point of view. In generally difficult and insecure situations, they are able to help others by showing the bright side of things or by pepping us up with a good dose of enthusiasm. They can even set out so enthusiastically that others will fall into step behind. This is especially due to an unconscious emotional identification, which Sagittarius uses to get "fired up." And so Moon-sign Sagittarians can come to the rescue in difficult situations, even though tact is not one of their stronger points, and even though they do not always read the future aright.

Owing to the urge to be continually doing something new and continually finding out new things, this Moon will frequently set itself such distant goals that they look more like castles in the air than anything else. Above all there can be an unshakable identification with certain aims and/or ideas: with a partly regressive energy the Moon becomes well entrenched in these ideas, while all remaining progressive energy is used to preach to others. Sagittarius needs to have something to advocate, and usually things can be kept (emotionally) in proportion. But if restrictions or inhibitions lead to the formation of *idées fixes* (fixed ideas which dominate the mind), then the person with Moon in Sagittarius will attempt to live according to certain insights which may be entirely devoid of practical value.

Moon in Sagittarius will also use the need to widen horizons (fire and mutable cross) as a means of dealing with uncertain situations. For example, this person may start a warm philosophical argument or talk about personal development; on the other hand, he may look inward in an attempt to extend personal insights or look outward by using the insights already won to expand the horizons of others. A positive response from one's circle of acquaintances can make one feel good, but it is unlikely that a negative response will cool the enthusiasm generated by the fire element and fueled by the mutable cross. Hence someone with the Moon in Sagittarius can often display more resolution than someone with the Sun there when it comes to bulldozing one's way through opposition. Achieving personal security is paramount.

MERCURY IN SAGITTARIUS

When this planet is in fire signs, the (from an archetypal point of view) completely objective influence receives a certain amount of subjective coloration, since fire is so egocentric. This coloration is most pronounced in the "investigative" sign Sagittarius. Owing to a need to understand the interrelationships and the sense of things (a fire characteristic), people with Mercury in Sagittarius will want to fit personal events into their philosophy of life. Therefore they will not always be able to face facts objectively but will try to bring them into agreement with current notions. They will make connections between facts intuitively, being convinced of a special hidden relationship.

People with Mercury in Sagittarius will, when temporarily under the influence of inner compulsions, endeavor to work out a philosophy of life and will try to live in accordance with it, however impossible the task may be. But, in any case, they will never feel that they have completed this task: a longing for expansion (fire) and a need for change and for something *more* (mutability) are too great for that. The way in which they assimilate experiences compels them to keep searching and asking questions. This is the way they live. The mutable cross induces individuals to come to terms with life by discovering connections, by resolving conflicts and by integrating everything into a whole. When Mercury in Sagittarius looks at the facts of human experience, it is with a view to making a synthesis.

What happens when these individuals turn outward? They will try to preach to others what they have found within. An expanded horizon will be projected on the external world. Hence Sagittarians are in essence good teachers, even though mutability and the associated periodic irruptions of unconscious factors cause them to cling to absolutes. To put it more simply, longing for certainty may make them overanxious to emphasize their own point of view (as if to convince self as well as others), and this may make them difficult to reason with. What Sagittarius says goes, and others would do well to accept it!

There is a good deal of animation about the way in which someone with Mercury in Sagittarius communicates. Moving along sweeping lines of thought, this sign can skip from one thing to another in such a way that it is hard to follow. The manner of speech and gesture is lively and sometimes stirring. These people are always ready to stand up for their opinion and will often display a tactless openness.

Normally those with Mercury in Sagittarius will live a life of searching, but if they allow themselves to be confined to the center of the mutable cross on the border between the conscious and the unconscious (so that they switch from one to the other without reaching the heights or depths of either), then their searching can petrify into a rigid ideology from which they never secede. When this psychic energy is obstructed, they will define their position come what may and can turn into extremely sectarian thinkers, the very opposite of the open and free "searchers for truth."

VENUS IN SAGITTARIUS

In Sagittarius the Venusian need of harmony and beauty, of comfort and security and of a love relationship is expressed in the manner of fire; that is to say, in a vivacious, warm, open-hearted and, above all, inconstant way. Beauty, harmony and love are sought not so much in the material as in the ideal realm. Sagittarius as a seeking sign is, generally speaking, only marginally concerned with the material world, and only then when it enters for a time the inward-looking phase of the mutable cross and all sorts of unconscious factors linked with the buried earth element begin to surface.

Venus in Sagittarius does a great deal of seeking, which means that someone with this position in the birth chart is often reputed to be unfaithful and eager to have affairs. Yet that is no more than one possibility; for if the partner is stimulating and both the man and the woman can lead a life full of change, the need for constant variety is satisfied within the union, and the individual with Venus in Sagittarius will never dream of deserting his or her partner for another. It is only when there is an obstruction to the deep-rooted longing for new things and for change that the desire to make fresh conquests begins to show itself.

A significant feature of Venus in Sagittarius is that close relationships, such as marriage, must form no barrier to the native's opportunities for personal development. People with Venus in Sagittarius have a name for being freedom-loving, but this must not be taken as meaning that they will never marry or cohabit. What it does mean is that they will always feel that their need for emotional and material security can be expressed in a Sagittarian manner.

Material things are relatively unimportant for this Venus, and a sense of security mainly comes from working on relationships, from being able to experience new things, and from being able to keep looking for ideals it is possible to share (fire and the mutable cross!). Beauty, too, is sought in spiritual values such as can be found in unspoiled nature. Ideals and philosophies are also things in which the cast of mind given by Venus in Sagittarius can find beauty and enchantment.

The person with Venus in Sagittarius can give a warm hand of fellowship to others and can express much love and affection. A marital union or in general any love bond is based more on ideals and a shared philosophy of life than on a partnership wallowing in material prosperity. But, if obstructed, the Venusian influence can exaggerate the urge to keep looking for *more* into too much wanting and the inability to be satisfied with any situation or relationship whatever. The ideal union is made so unobtainable that the native will keep on flitting from one superficial contact to another. There may be a certain amount of glamor in the number of "conquests" made, but otherwise they will be very hollow.

Venus in Sagittarius imparts the need for further development in relationships: Venus urges us not to lie back but to bring this vision to life—in partnership with others. If we follow the promptings, we will seek that ideal relationship in love or friendship into which all our warmth can be poured.

MARS IN SAGITTARIUS

With an energetic planet like Mars in such a mutable sign as Sagittarius, we can hardly expect anything other than the release of a great deal of power and a love of hard work. Because the cross is a mutable one, the industrious nature can find expression in both the inner and the outer areas of life. The desire to distinguish oneself from others and to express one's own individuality is very marked here. The element fire is always very egocentric and seeks to differentiate itself from others, while the mutable cross encourages the native to seek to integrate continually new experiences into both personality and theories. The native's own opinion, a personal claim to freedom and opportunities for development are pursued and defended with great ardor and enthusiasm. Mars in Sagittarius creates a need for the individual to distinguish himself from others by work and activities. It is immaterial whether this need is fulfilled by superior achievements (the sense of rivalry is great) or by being different from others in thought and outlook.

The person with Mars in Sagittarius may find it difficult to keep to one form of activity. Mars is compelled, so to speak, by the mutable cross to undertake too much—often with the object of making its presence felt. Idealistic aims can play a part here; but, above all, Mars must keep busy!

These natives can harness all their energies in the service of an ideal, but also in the service of unreal things once they get the idea in their heads. They are prepared to advocate a favorite cause with a good deal of aggression; not because they want to behave badly, but because it is easy for the natural aggression of Mars to come to the surface in a fire sign. Belligerent moments quickly pass, but often they find themselves having to pick up the broken pieces.

As already mentioned, personal freedom is highly prized by those with Mars in Sagittarius. We are not talking about licentiousness, but (as we saw with Venus) about the freedom to pursue our own path, to carry on with our development and to keep searching for new things. Active Mars will convert the seeking element in Sagittarius into immediate action. This may mean a love of travel, the endless lure of the wild blue yonder, or perhaps a desire to explore new dimensions in the psyche. But, if their energy is not allowed free expression, people with Mars here will be quick to abscond from the paternal home or to desert a partner simply because they do not wish to be tied down too tightly.

Anyone who has Mars in Sagittarius needs plenty of room for maneuver and development. The development can be an inner development provided they can give free rein to their own individuality.

JUPITER IN SAGITTARIUS

The planet representing the need of mankind for expansion—Jupiter—is very much at home in its own sign Sagittarius, which is everlastingly engaged in seeking new areas of opportunity. And so, when in Sagittarius, Jupiter is completely free to develop in its own way. Jupiter's craving for spiritual and religious values is brought out more strongly in the inquisitive sign Sagittarius. This craving finds expression in a fire manner, and, in addition, the mutable cross tends to combine and integrate everything the individual encounters. Therefore further development can occur in the direction of the religious, the ideal and the metaphysical, depending on the individual's attitude. More than that of any other planet, the influence of Jupiter will incite the native to look for significance with a captial S and to assess facts on the basis of their meaning in the greater whole. The native may look at life from a traditional religious point of view or perhaps from the point of view of more recent metaphysical conceptions, but, whichever point of view is adopted, he is certainly out to see things in a more comprehensive light than ordinary facts seem to shed on them.

This search for a more comprehensive picture of the cosmos inclines the person with Jupiter in Sagittarius to develop a vision by which he will do his level best to live. However, unlike the person with Mars in Sagittarius, he will not devote himself to the vision's attainment—he regards it as self-evident and one would be hard put to divert him from it. He will judge things and react to situations in accordance with its dictates, fortified by an inner "faith." This "faith" is not confined to spiritual and metaphysical values: convictions on social and political matters can also harden into unshakable tenets.

Nevertheless, the individual who has Jupiter in Sagittarius will always be on the watch for fresh values to integrate. What he would really like to do is to gather so much wisdom that he can afford a gentle smile while shaking a sage and "fatherly" head over the foolish antics of the world. If this search for genuine wisdom is obstructed, this Jupiter may still pretend to find it and may be content with boasting and self-conceit. Should one settle for some narrow vision, this Jupiter may judge matters from a personal viewpoint, or will see them in a highly colored light, or may try to prove himself right by ramming personal opinions down other people's throats. But, whatever the case, one does need to construct some image of the world, either secular or religious.

The Jovian Sagittarian is happiest when producing from within an all-embracing and idealistic world-view in which every fact and phenomenon has its relationships and its proper place.

Judgments and reactions will be guided by an inner vision (whether conscious or unconscious) regardless of viability: the vision is *his* vision (fire) and he is intent on its expansion (mutability).

SATURN IN SAGITTARIUS

The planet of "learning through pain" invariably works in such a way in the element fire as to inhibit the love of life in some fashion, and yet at the same time it creates the need to enjoy life in deep drafts. It gives a desire for uncomplicated joy, such as Saturn in fire can supply only after much patient suffering. The unbridled, enterprising quality of fire has little in common with the controlled inward-looking nature of the planet Saturn, and Saturn is certainly not at home in the expansive sign Sagittarius. On the other hand, Saturn in this placement does need to let the ego be formed in a Sagittarian manner—but the going is tough. Therefore, when occupied by Saturn, this sign may be a weak spot in the horoscope.

The weakness will reveal itself in various ways. Saturn in Sagittarius may bring on an anxiety neurosis with the fear of not being a success in life, and it may oppose the expansive and horizon-widening influence of Sagittarius, discouraging any search for what is new. A gnawing desire to investigate things remains, however (this is, after all, still part of the makeup of the psyche!), and these individuals may set off on a quest more ardently than would one with the Sun, Mars or Jupiter in this sign—if only to prove that they are really "living." Thus Saturn in Sagittarius subjects can make ill-considered travel plans or can kick over the traces in no uncertain manner, yet with distinct twinges of conscience. Eventually they learn to recognize their own limitations, though not until they have had to take a good many hard knocks.

Internally, people with Saturn in Sagittarius can look for ideals and for some philosophy of life they can use for the demarcation process that will help in the formation of conscious awareness. This entails a risk that they will adopt dogmatic stances over some pet theory simply because the ego needs to have a sense of certainty, when instead they should be waiting for genuine inner "knowing."

Externally, these natives must, of necessity, go through many adventures; it is the nature of the mutable cross to assimilate experience. The problem here is that the mutable cross has more to do with transitions between one thing and another than with solid facts. The practical hard work of the earth signs is lacking in the fire element because concreteness and realism are not essential to ideals and goals; yet it is this very practicality that the influence of Saturn makes so important for character formation.

With Saturn in Sagittarius, the wish to make the most of life can occasionally lead these natives to physical or mental extremes in expressing this sign. But after they have fallen down a few times, the influence of Saturn can assert itself to temper rashness and to help them live life with greater insight.

URANUS, NEPTUNE AND PLUTO IN SAGITTARIUS

When we come to consider the planets which affect people in general, we can say that the tendency to break form and the need to be original (Uranus), the desire to refine form, to tear it from its moorings and to make it universal (Neptune), and the craving for power, confrontation and the transcendence of form (Pluto), will manifest themselves with considerable fire and enthusiasm in the sign Sagittarius. The need for expansion and for getting the most out of life play their part here, so that the planetary influences are quite recognizable in both the inner and the outer life. But, as they lie mostly outside human control, they can manifest themselves in both their most positive and their most negative forms.

And so the signature left by Neptune on an era can be written in two entirely different styles. On the one hand there is the impulse to encourage the disassociation of form in a bid to reach far horizons beyond mundane things. This is a direct cause of the present-day drug problem: people hope that the psychedelic scene will put them in touch with new experiences and visionary revelations. On the other hand, and at the same time, there is a growing realization even among scientists that matter is completely different from what has been thought. Individuals and groups are raising their voices ever more loudly in support of immaterial and spiritual values. The displacement of the horizon to somewhere beyond the tangible and the perceptible is one expression of the link-breaking planet Neptune in the link-seeking sign Sagittarius. In both cases we are collectively looking for what lies *behind* form, for an idea in which form and content stand in a wholly different relationship to one another, and the distinction between them becomes blurred. It is the same underlying motive at work in the drug problems and in the breaking of new ground in science, even though the modes of manifestation are totally different. The image of a planetary era created by the passage of that planet through a given zodiac sign is elaborated later on by the generation that grows up under this planetary position—because they are the children of their time.

Uranus and Pluto will also have an internal and an external effect when they are in Sagittarius. The connections and conflicts of concepts and ideas begin to be seen more clearly. And so Uranus holds the promise of new and original insights, while Pluto in this sign extends and perfects them, but not without power struggles both in the individual and in the surrounding world.

CHAPTER FOUR

PLANETS IN THE ELEMENT EARTH

1. FIXED EARTH: TAURUS

SUN IN TAURUS

The way in which Sun in Taurus people find it most satisfactory to express their nature is by creating security in material things. Their world is that of concrete reality and sensory perception. Because they belong to the fixed cross, not only do they keep a firm grip on the physical world but they set themselves to assimilate the impressions and impulses which come from it. Thinking is always down to earth.

Thanks to the fixed cross influence, Taureans stand in great need of security—seemingly much more so than do members of the other earth signs. The fixed cross dredges up many unconscious factors into the conscious mind, and this can make for a sense of insecurity. A consciousness that is already sold on security (earth) can easily come to lay even greater emphasis on it. Hence natives of Taurus often have a reputation for being possessive and materialistic; this is not because they take to materialism on ideological grounds, but because they feel safer that way. So, too, they find it hard to change their current situations or to move on to something new. Their reactions come only after long and deep thought. That is why Taurus folk take so long to respond and can persevere in a given life style or situation. The disadvantage of this behavior is that many opportunities are lost through a lack of flexibility and because the native reacts too slowly.

On the other hand, few signs are so reliable and solid as Taurus. Due to their tenacity, Taurus natives can carry on the battle for lost causes and, thanks to the fixed cross influence, will sometimes save the day too. This mode of assimilation always brings the unconscious inferior function to the surface, and the inferior function in the case of earth is the element fire. Thus a note of insecurity is introduced into the conscious attitude toward material things; there is an unconscious tendency to continue to see or to discover possibilities (unreal to the conscious mind) in something that could in fact have nothing more to offer. The longing for security makes the Taurus subject look for reassurance in what is tried and tested. Taurus tends to trust the familiar.

Owing to a cautiousness and need to let everything come out from within, the Taurean (as a fixed sign individual) is slow to make a move. But once under way, Taurus is hard to stop. Once having set a course in a certain direction, this sign devotes all energies to traveling that way; hence the concentrated power displayed and the great output of steady work. One could aptly picture Taurus as one of those grand old steam locomotives making a thundering onrush over well-made levels.

The search for security can make one rather conservative. Too much change easily puts one off stroke. In addition, as already said, Taurus looks for security mainly in concrete and material things where he feels most at home—in the things which can be seen, heard and handled. The need to develop on the material plane can express itself in countless ways. On the one hand Taurus likes to own things; on the other hand this sign likes to process raw materials as a form of self-expression. Artistry, stylistics, "making things nice," are all Taurus characteristics, and so are caring for plants and animals.

Even abstract matters will be turned into something "material" or "real" by the Taurean to enable the sign type to come to grips with them. An idea has no value unless it holds good in practice. Although flickers from the hidden fire element light up many possibilities, Taurus will consider only one possibility at a time. "How," he may ask, "can I be expected to lay a fourth course of bricks when the third course is not yet in place?" The abstract and the ideal must be part and parcel of solid reality.

The marriage bond is no abstract concept for Taurus. To the Taurean wife, for example, her husband is very much a personal possession, and the fact that she is his "owner" gives her a sense of security. Anything that threatens this touches a raw nerve. She will have him under her watchful eye and, unless he is prepared to face her jealous rage, he will let her keep him in line.

If the need for security is obstructed in any way, Taurus can overcompensate. For instance, there can be an obsession with acquiring material wealth (a fortune in gems, say), the pursuit of pleasure and of whatever titillates the senses (including sexual overindulgence), the reckless defense of personal property and the unwillingness to share the family circle with others. But if normal development if free to take place, the individual can mature into an artistic, creative, amiable and thoughtful person who loves and respects all that lives; into someone who sets an example to others in the simple and natural enjoyment of earthly life.

MOON IN TAURUS

The element earth seeks security in what is concrete and perceptible, but the Moon too is looking for security—for emotional security—and so there is a double emphasis on security, especially where material things are concerned. Because of the fixed cross, impulses from the unconscious will continually impinge on the conscious mind and place the ego under pressure. This has an undermining effect that will increase the longing for settled security—just as we found with the Sun in Taurus.

When people with Moon in Taurus find themselves in a difficult situation, they prefer to start looking at the solid facts of the case, that is to say, at what *is*. They have little inclination to take things any further than this, either in thought or in deed, because it would carry them out of their emotional depths. Owing to the fixed cross influence, they look for something substantial to cling to, and so those with Moon in Taurus may appear to be very reserved in emotional responses, especially in situations where they are not very sure of themselves.

Because Moon in Taurus encourages people to keep their feet on the ground, this is what they will usually do, though in many different ways. Concentration on the concrete material world and the pleasure of being involved in it, will mean that we often find

Taureans enjoying the good things of life. Creature comforts are always important whether they be great or small, and they like to shape their surroundings and fill them with beauty. They may do this in any number of ways: by tending a garden full of plants (for lovely surroundings delighting the senses), by cooking fine meals, by exercising artistic talents in painting, sculpting, modeling and the like, by an interest in personal adornment, the preparation (or, if necessary the purchasing) of perfumes, etc. The nub of the matter is that Taureans feel good when they have plenty to keep them occupied in the physical, everyday world, the world of the five traditional senses. Any hindrance leads to overcompensations in the form of an excessive love of sensual pleasures, of luxury and sloth, and in the form of conservatism bordering on miserliness.

The family is very important as a source of security, and these natives will certainly care for it; there is a danger however that spouse or children will be treated as property and there can be some violent reactions from the otherwise placid Taureans (quarreling and strife are alarmingly unsettling factors for Taurus in the ordinary way for several reasons). Frequently these individuals (even more than those with Sun in Taurus, since we are dealing here with unconscious feelings of satisfaction and dissatisfaction!) will find it difficult to let the children leave home as they approach adulthood.

And so the way in which the world is approached is strongly influenced by the need for security. The presence of the fixed cross means that whatever is felt is felt very deeply. This means that these individuals can prove exacting in times of crisis, but it is also a guarantee of loyalty when they find something after their own heart. Like Sun in Taurus, the Moon in this sign makes for great stability and reliablity in such cases.

MERCURY IN TAURUS

A planet as active and prone to make contacts as Mercury has difficulty in expressing its fleetly executed shifts in such a reserved, inward-looking and calm sign as Taurus. The experiences encountered by Mercury in Taurus are set in order according to tried-and-tested patterns firmly rooted in reality. Life is regarded from a rather materialistic standpoint. Everything is reduced to the perceptible, and possibilities are seldom taken beyond what can be realized in the physical world. The native would rather have nothing to do with the "unreal": anything that is inexplicable in terms of the five senses can only aggravate the sense of insecurity. When an individual with Mercury in Taurus is concerned with parapsychology or the occult, for example, he will always try to make these phenomena as concrete as possible.

However, after a while the game is spoiled by the element fire that, in earth signs, lies buried in the unconscious. When the fixed cross brings this element to the surface, Mercury in Taurus can pass through phases in which the mind tends to lose touch with reality, so the native gives credence to the wildest and most improbable theories and tales, and peppers the thinking with all kinds of superstition.

The manner in which the person with Mercury in Taurus communicates is calm and cautious; the policy is one of wait-and-see because one wants to play for keeps. Before moving into action, Mercury thinks carefully about what to do or say, and likes to know what is expected. Therefore Mercury is good at the sort of business management which relies on thoughtful planning. The actual decision making is usually best left to others, since Mercury in Taurus is inclined to stick to the old routine, trusting the familiar.

VENUS IN TAURUS

As the psychic factor representing our need for comfort and safety, the planet Venus is really at home in Taurus, since it can express a desire for security so well in this security-building sign. If this desire is overemphasized, it may well seek security in the total ownership of the loved one. Venus will prepare a warm and cosy little love nest—and make the loved one stay there! It is no good pleading that theirs was a casual affair, or that there is no longer anything between them; Venus in Taurus will teach the lover differently.

Although the need for love is great, the potential partner is carefully studied; for influences express themselves in Taurus calmly, guardedly and sometimes very patiently. Venus in Taurus takes a long time to make an open commitment, for the fixed cross demands a full assimilation of all feelings and emotions; but once formed, the bond will hardly ever be broken, as the need for security quickly comes to the fore to tighten and strengthen it.

As might be expected, the concrete and the material play a part in love and friendship. The native will readily share the good things in life with a friend or partner. Considerable importance is attached to all sorts of little (and not so little) luxuries and indulgences. If the psychic energy is obstructed in any way, this can lead to an overemphasis on these things so that there is a love of pleasure, and friendships are struck up on the basis of material factors.

The need for beauty and harmony with which to bathe the senses can find expression in two ways in Taurus: inwardly in the great need for peace and, more materially, in artistry and creative handiwork. The fine arts and gracious and sensuous living are Venus-in-Taurus characteristics. A feeling for matter and form (earth) and a need for harmony (Venus) make the individual suited to many things which have to do with shape and style.

MARS IN TAURUS

The need to stand apart from others and to appear aggressive is heavily overlaid in Taurus by the longing for peace and safety peculiar to this sign. So, Mars in Taurus people will not be hasty to break friendships and relationships. The safety they experience makes them loathe to break free. Nevertheless, they will fight tooth and nail to defend what is dear, whether people or things.

Energy is not so directly released in the inward-looking sign Taurus. The fixed cross invests considerable energy in unconscious processes, and so those with Mars in Taurus do not give the impression of being so full of life. All the same, Mars in Taurus packs enough energy to move mountains; all that is needed is to find some way of rousing him. Once the will to action has been wakened, these people are virtually unstoppable: the fixed cross gives a *fixed* purpose—indeed perseverance is almost proverbial. But the initial impulse must come from outside.

The urge to prove themselves also comes from a need to feel secure. Whenever someone with perseverence is needed to handle routine chores, you can't do better than hand them over to someone with Mars in Taurus! Actively working with materials is very satisfying, and these natives' bodily strength and powers of resistance are extremely great.

Once the aggression of Mars in Taurus is aroused (which can easily happen if anyone threatens to take or harm what the individual regards as personal property), then the martian energy will rage with unconfined fury. Instead of making sure that everything is safe and sound, Mars will very likely employ fearsome physical energy in smashing everything up. The fits of temper of an otherwise peace-loving martian Taurean can be violent!

JUPITER IN TAURUS

Jupiter's need to increase, to make space and, in a word, to be expansive, operates here within the framework of the Taurean desire for comfort and safety; which means that there is a good chance of material security being sought in the form of possessions. When in Taurus, Jupiter is inclined to work with the concrete and the material; and in obeying the urge to place facts and events in a large-scale setting does so in as useful and as practical a manner as possible, in spite of the fact that Jupiter is not naturally so down-to-earth. The involvement with spiritual and religious values is also grafted onto the need for security, and so the attitude to such matters is conservative.

Whereas in other signs Jupiter mainly produces spiritual values which will give a basis for a philosophy of life but without overmuch regard to the character of those values, in Taurus every effort is made to make that basis solid.

Every now and then, disturbing unconscious factors surface into consciousness via the fixed cross influence. And so, if the Jovian energy is blocked or impeded, the search for security will be stepped up, especially in the plane where the element earth feels safe—the plane of matter. The individual may go mad about collecting and hoarding things but never feel satisfied with the result; it can be justified by calling it a nest egg.

Owing to the effect of the fixed cross, spiritual values can come under the influence of the unconscious fire element, so that the need to widen one's horizon, typical of Jupiter, is given a boost. For this position of Jupiter, that can mean adopting the most fanciful and unsubstantial beliefs, to which the individual holds just as firmly as he does to the more material side of life. It is not easy to dissuade someone with Jupiter in Taurus from a special "belief," to which he can hold with childlike simplicity because it makes him feel secure. In extreme cases, we will see a fanaticism minus the normally friendly approach of Taurus.

To sum up, both the spiritual needs and the urge to expand are governed by a desire to preserve what exists and to win some form of security both spiritual and material.

SATURN IN TAURUS

Since Saturn represents our weak spot, it will create great sensitivity on the question of safety and comfort when placed in Taurus. The process by which consciousness is formed has a Taurean background, and this background suggests concrete interests (earth) and has an intense manner of assimilation (the fixed cross), so that unconscious and inner desires prevail. The uncertainty attendant on the invasion of factors via the fixed cross means that Saturn can readily give rise to overcompensation in all sorts of different ways. One thing that may happen is a great concentration on material values paired with an interest in spiritual things (e.g., a liking for forms and ceremonies), and this search for assurance can be even more compulsive than it was for Jupiter in Taurus. The Taurean need for security aggravates the equally great uncertainty and vulnerability of Saturn.

Another, and common, type of overcompensation is to renounce material values and, in extreme cases, to give all personal possessions away in order to live as a "brother of poverty" or a recluse—mainly because the natives fear that any attachment to worldly goods will confront them with the weak side of the nature.

The constructive ability of Saturn is great, however, once these people learn how to live with this weak side of the nature. The natives will then find that Saturn in Taurus will enable them to adopt a very solid and reliable pattern of life, within the confines of which they are free to develop with feelings of inner security.

URANUS, NEPTUNE AND PLUTO IN TAURUS

The tendency to break forms and the urge to be original (Uranus), the need to refine form, to unravel it and make it universal (Neptune), and the need for power, confrontation and transcendence (Pluto), express themselves in a quiet and conservative way when these planets are in Taurus. Uranus will not be so ready to reveal its iconoclastic nature when in this sign as it is when in the other signs, because security, being the essence of Taurus, is bound to color the planet's influence to some extent.

Neptune in Taurus tends to blur the outlines of fixed forms. Seen positively, when borders are dissolved one has the opportunity to see further than usual. The negative side is that physical reality may become shrouded in such a mist that contact with the concrete is lost, and there are no longer any fixed points of reference because of the sense of uncertainty projected from the unconscious mind.

Power struggles will not break out so readily if Pluto is in Taurus but, when they do arise, they are likely to be long lasting. Among those things which are represented by Pluto, are the contents of the unconscious and especially those things which have been repressed. These contents come slowly to the surface in Taurus. As a matter of fact, they put the native under continual pressure but, because Taurus needs to feel secure and because difficulty is experienced in recognizing imponderables, they can be held at bay for a long time. However, once they break through, the situation can become chronic, and everything becomes wavering and uncertain.

2. MUTABLE EARTH: VIRGO

SUN IN VIRGO

As in the previous sign, the Sun in Virgo is mainly oriented toward solid, tangible reality. An individual with the Sun in Virgo will feel most at ease in the world of the five senses. Whatever cannot be seen, heard, smelled, tasted or touched is either denied or else made as concrete as possible.

Experiences are assimilated after the manner of the mutable cross. In other words, there is a strong tendency to come to terms with things by taking them to pieces before integrating them. In obeying this tendency, Virgo will set to work in a very concrete way to insure that the disintegration and integration serve some practical purpose.

As a means of assimilation, the mutable cross is dualistic, and its dualism is evident in the sign Virgo. The mutable cross has a need to build bridges—both between the conscious and the unconscious and between situations and people. As the reader will see, the bridge building can be inside or outside the individual but, in any case, it does introduce a note of service into the Virgo makeup. Also, because the Virgo mind tends to concentrate on form, people born under this sign often like to "save the day" (to preserve the shape of things).

In every situation, the natives try to serve the world (and even more to serve themselves) by reconciling opposites, fostering understanding between others to solve difficulties. By so doing, they can adopt a completely neutral position and forget themselves. Nevertheless, we should not fall into the trap of thinking Virgos are self-sacrificing and idealistic: this mode of expression is necessary if they are to fulfill what is in their deepest being. Should Virgos lack opportunity to put themselves in someone else's position (but only temporarily, for after all the mutable cross is by definition "movable"!) and to treat the information gained in a concrete, combinative, integrating and problem-solving way, they would feel uncomfortable. Being of service to others is a reflection of the way their minds work—it supports their ego, which is why the service is frequently rendered in a somewhat neutral and impersonal manner.

The mutable cross is always looking for fresh stimuli, either external or internal. But the Sun in an earth sign, which craves security, has no intention of setting out on new adventures at the drop of a hat. In certain circumstances this can lead to overcompensation.

The feeling for facts and concrete things, combined with a need for change, incites these natives to take interest in a multiplicity of facts, to approach data in a down-to-earth fashion, and to look at it from every angle. However, the vision and the ability to take an overall view so characteristic of the element fire (though often with a striking lack of appreciation of solid facts) is completely missing from Virgoan makeup. Virgos find it easy to analyze but not so easy to synthesize. They have an eye for detail, and not just *one* detail; it is remarkable how many small points they can take in at one time when dealing with practical matters.

Because of an eye for detail and a tendency to jump from one point to another, people with Sun in Virgo have a reputation for being fussy, fastidious in housekeeping and even prudish. They sometimes give the imprssion that they live for nothing else than to keep scrubbing and polishing. Yet this is completely untrue. These natives have an overwhelming desire to bridge over difficulties (mutable cross influence) in as practical a manner as possible (earth). Also, they like to clear away any small obstacles which might prove a hindrance to others. Hence it is not so much that they are suffering from an inborn "tidiness mania" as that they have a need to keep relating things to one another in a useful and concrete way, and this often involves a close scrutiny of surroundings and the removal of material and/or spiritual rubbish. It goes without saying that they will sometimes go too far in tidying up "loose ends" instead of making allowance for them, and so Virgo mutability may move them into a state of alienation from themselves or others. While we are on this last point it is worth mentioning that the apparent detachment from the ego (the ego always puts service to others on a neutral basis) many mean that no one can ever penetrate to the real person.

If the Virgo energy is obstructed, overcompensation can turn the originally neat Virgo into an unrecognizable slut or sloven (they always retain a *sense* of neatness however) with little care for decency, and so on. The overcompensation consists either in the denial of his or her own nature or in laying undue stress on it, so that the Virgo characteristics become distorted.

MOON IN VIRGO

The unconscious emotional behavior is chiefly concentrated on solid, material security (earth) but acts in a serviceable, problem-solving and integrating way (mutable cross). This means that the Moon in Virgo individual often gives the impression of being simple, modest and undemanding, because one of the first concerns is the wants and wishes of others. This is how Virgo builds up a sense of security. So if we hinder someone with Moon in Virgo (or the Sun in Virgo for that matter) from helping to straighten things out for us, we deprive them of a source of inner satisfaction. Where emotional reactions are directly concerned, the person with Moon in Virgo will respond in an earth manner in the first instance; that is to say, calmly and coolly, and rather cautiously and passively too. The mutable cross influence inclines the Moon to view the situation from all sides before doing anything about it. The response may be delayed but it will be deliberate or well considered.

In the spontaneous, unconscious reaction to situations, small, concrete things can play an important part, and without the individual always being aware of it. A person with this placement of the Moon can therefore excel in matters of style, without perhaps knowing why. The automatic reaction is generally critical and analytic due to the need to make things as beautiful and harmonious as possible and because Virgo likes to be practical and purposeful. In this Virgo can be really very inventive. The mutable earth gives a liking for change, while the unconscious fire sign influence occasionally breaks through with its visionary ideas. Nevertheless, the individual with the Moon in Virgo reacts calmly and rather conservatively.

The need to serve makes both Sun and the Moon in Virgo people extremely suited to positions in which they have others under their care, e.g., training them or nursing them. This is particularly true of those with Moon in Virgo, because it gives them satisfaction and reassurance deep down in their unconscious minds: one of the means of expression by which the mutable cross takes shape on the material plane.

The emotional response in various situations may seem cool, but inside there is little coolness; everything is feverishly examined from all sides, but it is not until the examination is complete that the mask of reserve is dropped and an opinion is expressed. However, by the time these natives are ready to express an opinion, the situation has changed and they have a fresh pile of data to consider—perhaps not all the time, but more often than not. And so this analytical approach has led others to say that the person with the Moon in Virgo lets their head rule the heart. Yet, if ever the inferior element fire flames through, sudden "visions" can also emerge and the Virgo Moon can come out with something completely at variance with the normal manner of expression.

The need to mean something to others, however unassumingly, makes those with Moon in Virgo very sensitive to criticism. They are quick to take this as evidence that their services are unwanted, and feel very insecure. One of two reactions follows: either they act the perfectionist right from the start, leaving nothing to chance and attending to every small detail, or they withdraw into a shell (somewhat regressively) without forgetting what has been said. The whole course of events and everything connected will be examined all over again and assimilated.

There is considerable turmoil going on inside the outwardly seeming calm and collected Moon-in-Virgo native. The mutable cross is naturally restless and always looking for something new; hence the native, too, is constantly on the search both internally and externally but, since Virgo is an earth sign, the search will be for some sort of solid reality.

MERCURY IN VIRGO

The thinking processes of people with Mercury in Virgo (the way in which we marshal, classify and analyze facts) are carried out under the influence of the element earth; that is to say, in as functional and concrete a manner as possible and with an eye to practical use and physical reality. The mutable energy of Virgo is in perfect keeping with the restless nature of Mercury. Mercury prompts us to persevere in the search for new things or in the attempt to see old things from fresh angles and to reassess material accordingly. The mutable energy of Virgo is also characterized by a need for change. Above all, down-to-earth Virgos want to have facts and figures arranged in as authentic and as clear a manner as possible, and this is a task in which Mercury is happy to cooperate. Mercury finds it exceptionally easy to show both its best and its worst sides in Virgo.

Mercury in Virgo, then, distinguishes itself by the power to analyze, to set facts in order and categorize them, to study and learn. But Mercury in Virgo lacks the vision of the element fire and will usually fail to see the overall significance of the patterns made, in spite of the occasional incursions of the inferior element fire from out of the unconscious mind.

The individual whose birth chart has the analytical and plan-making planet Mercury in the analytical and plan-making sign Virgo will soon attract attention by a methodical approach, practical logic and an ability to make sharp distinctions both in thinking and formulating.

In ordinary social intercourse, people with Mercury in Virgo will want to serve others. There are various ways in which they can do this. For example, they may strive to extend the boundaries of useful knowledge or look for practical applications of specialized research. However, this is not to say that they are enthusiastic communicators: their main interest is in meaning something to others. Because of the mutable cross influence, they do not "clam up" entirely, but a definite approach must be made before they will divulge information.

The use of gesture by individuals with Mercury in Virgo is restrained, and they choose words carefully and well. They usually make an impression of being stolid but, as with any of the planets when in Virgo, there is a lively if matter-of-fact mentality.

If obstructed, the psychic energy can display various reactions: either there is an overemphasis on small details in an attempt to deal with the sense of uncertainty, so that the person becomes a hair-splitter, or else there is a great attachment to established fact (the security of earth!) and an unwillingness to change, so one may be characterized by dogmation and rigidity.

Normally, Mercury in Virgo likes to concentrate on working out ways of improving existing situations and on solving problems; especially by undertaking useful research, by analyzing, by lending a helping hand and by making useful contacts. Given half a chance, all sorts of profitable ideas and inventions can spring up in this fertile brain.

VENUS IN VIRGO

The Venusian need for comfort and security in emotional and in material things agrees well with the down-to-earth character of Virgo; but, although the earth element influence in Virgo seems to make for passivity and a policy of wait and see, the mutable cross influence makes for busy involvement in anything useful. Security is experienced in bringing people and things together and in helping the partner. The analytical ability of the person with Venus in Virgo, coupled with a slow and deliberate type of response, makes it hard to express warm or spontaneous love. The initial approach to affairs of the heart seems to be rather intellectual, but this does not mean a complete absence of passion. A human need for warmth and security is certainly there, but it is expressed in a practical and coolly appraising way. Venus in Virgo has a special liking for small, pretty things and not so much for an ostentatious show.

Making friends is often preferred to falling madly in love. Venus in Virgo creates the feeling that being in love has little to do with reality and that one can build better on friendship. This very practical attitude can brand the individual as devoid of emotion; however, emotion is there in plenty; it is the manner in which it is revealed to the outside world that is not always so tempestuous.

The need to enjoy beauty and harmony can lead to creative activities in the arts—as was true of Venus in Taurus. However, in this case there is more emphasis on what is practical and serviceable. Inwardly, beauty is much appreciated, but the native may find it hard to put feelings into words.

If Venus in Virgo does not have the opportunity to make itself useful in a relationship or to feel that its contribution is being appreciated, overcompensations may result: either there is an even greater emphasis on service and usefulness, or the native becomes cross-grained and ready to complain loudly at every little thing. What suits Venus in Virgo best is to be valued for helpfulness in a relationship, and to be allowed to show and receive friendship without any great fuss and bother, which Venus here is ill equipped to handle. Left to its own devices, Venus in Virgo is well able to reconcile differences and to pour oil on troubled waters.

MARS IN VIRGO

The wish to assert one's independence is expressed here in a Virgo manner, that is to say, analytically and in a matter-of-fact sort of way. The energy of Mars is employed to emphasize this "difference" from others in the exercise of the native's skills. These natives will not easily be satisfied with their performances, but will take positive steps to improve so work is as efficient and as professional as possible. Rather less pleasingly, they can turn analytical search-lights on others instead of within. Then they become the archcritics who pounce on every fault while upsetting others with silly details. Since Mars energizes any activity in which it is engaged, trifles can be blown out of proportion.

Because it is in Virgo, Mars will need to stress its individuality in a concrete and practical manner. Dutifulness, perseverence in dotting even the smallest i's, and a determination to stop errors creeping in can make people with Mars in Virgo valued members of any work force, provided they are free to use their energy (otherwise they will become self-assertive and start competing with others in order to "prove themselves"). People with Mars in Virgo can produce exceptionally accurate and painstaking work. And because Virgo is a mutable sign, there is an incentive to keep on learning new things, to connect and analyze, all within a limited and somewhat materialistic framework. They can be methodical in a provocative way—even services can be rendered aggressively—but they feel impelled to be useful if only to distinguish themselves from others.

Due to the need to be continually occupied with new things, once they have a secure base the people with Mars in Virgo will persevere until they have reached the bottom of a problem. Thus they are invaluable helpers in any active investigation or in finding a practical application for its results.

The martian power of accomplishment tends to be restrained by the caution and passivity of the element earth; although, owing to the influence of the mutable cross, more outwardly than inwardly. Nevertheless, the subdued and controlled energy can still be put to good use and, with this placement of the planet, there is hardly any wastage of energy except on the odd occasions when the inferior element fire breaks through. However, if the native does not take care, too much energy will be expended on trifles.

The aggressiveness of the native can express itself in sharp words, since Virgo knows how to find the most stinging rejoinders for an angry Mars to use. Mars here is not the easiest to conduct negotiations with as Virgo is quite capable of seizing on every detail, and this is behavior that grows worse in the event of overcompensation.

JUPITER IN VIRGO

As an expansive influence in the psyche, Jupiter is in its detriment in Virgo, since it is restricted to expansion in the concrete, the practical and the analytical realm, and then chiefly in matters of detail. Now, that is precisely what for Jupiter has little value; yet it is the background to the Jovian activities in this placement. Obviously, something has to give here. The forming of spiritual and religious beliefs and the viewing of facts and events in a wider context than usual, require the power of synthesis rather than the power of analysis. But here in Virgo the expansiveness of Jupiter is employed in multiplying those details so beloved by the element earth. The religious feelings are reduced to a sense of duty, and the native will shoulder all sorts of responsibility, but there is hardly a trace of the fiery idealism so characteristic of the planet.

We saw how with Mars in Virgo services were often rendered in a belligerent way. Well, something of the sort is also true with Jupiter in this sign; not, we hasten to add, because the native needs to prove or measure self against others, but because of a strong desire to gain confidence by relating people, facts and things to one another, and by helping others. The longing for spiritual and religious verities may well mean that a "higher value" will be ascribed to relief work, analysis and service; and the native will try to justify involvement in these activities by offering as broad (Jupiter) an analysis (Virgo) as possible of the individuals or the situations concerned.

The sheer joy of living, which is inherent in Jupiter, is tempered when the planet is in Virgo, even though the mutable cross influence does encourage the native to go in search of it. If the Jovian energy is obstructed, it will force an outlet for itself somewhere: perhaps in the form of persistent meddlesomeness which intentionally hampers the endeavors of others, or perhaps by putting service to others on another footing—by working for some practical ideal like feeding the poor, say, or aiding the Third World. However, everything is governed by the desire to expand and by the search for a Virgo-type perfection.

SATURN IN VIRGO

Just as it was in the sign Taurus, Saturn in Virgo is especially vulnerable on the material plane (earth), but this vulnerability is reduced to some extent by the mutable cross giving the ability to see both sides of any question. All the same, the Virgo concentration on material things from a practical standpoint (and the desire to fulfill a useful role in life) does become a sensitive issue when Saturn is in this sign. Although there is a need to feel useful, the native is often convinced that he is not being useful enough or even that his efforts are to no avail. Naturally, this can lead to overcompensation: to anxiety, frustration and discomfort both mental and physical. Not infrequently, the person with Saturn in Virgo will become very obsequious and will volunteer to help in all sorts of little ways, and yet blame himself inwardly for having landed so much to do.

Also, although an analytical and practical approach to others, facts and events is very thorough and conscientious, these people shrink from turning the spotlight on themselves for this is a weak point. True, they will have to do so in order to grow in awareness, but they risk becoming hypercritical of self and subservient to others. The fondness for analysis accentuates the mental side of life, so that Saturn in Virgo is constantly sifting things in order to come to terms with the environment.

Nevertheless, with Saturn here a solid foundation can be laid for the development of the personality, since the natives repeatedly pass through many small phases until they have learned to cope with them. Now, if they carry the analysis of self and others to extremes, a sense of unity will be completely lost, and they can suddenly be plunged into a deep crisis when the lost sense of unity emerges in the midst of diversity as the influence of the inferior fire element temporarily makes itself felt via the mutable cross. They will perceive something grander than ever before, and this may enable them to get their vulnerability into perspective.

URANUS, NEPTUNE AND PLUTO IN VIRGO

The tendency to take fixed forms apart and to reassemble them in original ways (Uranus), the need to refine forms, to disassociate them and to make them universal (Neptune), and the need for power, confrontation and transcendence of form (Pluto), are channeled by Virgo into the area of solid, material considerations, though not to the same extent as when those planets are in Taurus. Virgo's membership of the mutable cross makes for considerable activity behind the apparent passivity of earth. Uranian originality and moldbreaking may well express on the physical plane in useful renovations and reforms, but without the dutifulness we associate with Virgo. Neptune, too, will operate on the physical plane to realize its ideals. However, the dangerous side of Neptune shows itself in Virgo by creating chaos. The influence of this planet creeps over things like a poison gas cloud: in this instance a fog of technical details may hide from researchers the extent to which their work is causing environmental pollution.

On the other hand, the forms introduced by Uranus in Virgo can be developed and championed by Pluto in Virgo, with fresh ground broken in the field of practical reforms and the introduction of new analytical methods (both in the physical sciences and in psychoanalysis). When Pluto is in Virgo, we may expect the development of power struggles in these areas, both at the time and in succeeding decades as the generation born with this placement reaches maturity.

3. CARDINAL EARTH: CAPRICORN

SUN IN CAPRICORN

As in the other earth signs, the Sun in Capricorn encourages the desire for physical security; however, the mode of operation is different since Capricorn belongs to the cardinal cross. The native's attitude to life is extravert, not so much from a need to project the personality as from a need to make his world secure—with and/or for others. Since he belongs to an earth sign, he will not so readily take the initiative, preferring to remain in the background until incited to action from without (the cardinal cross being so tightly geared to what goes on outside).

In order to make the valued outer world as safe as possible, individuals with Sun in Capricorn will work long and hard (often in the background) to formulate regulations, structures and controls. Faithfulness to goals is remarkable, even though it may take years to reach it.

Formulating rules in order to preserve the environment can be done in many ways. A person need not join the government; many less ambitious avenues are open to him. Sun in Capricorn encourages the conscious mind to become very much involved in the outside world of physical reality. Therefore, these natives look for security there and, if they do not find it, they endeavor to create it. They can be very persistent and will wait calmly for the opportunity to take the next step toward achieving an objective.

The rather conservative nature of the earth element means that Capricorn natives are unlikely to become great reformers but will, rather, become bringers of order within existing patterns. In so doing they may appear to be very individualistic and independent, but this is only partly true. Certainly, earth Sun sign natives are not hail-fellow-well-met with everybody and may easily pass as loners; yet, in fact, the cardinal cross influence makes them extremely dependent deep down—both on people and on things—and they are sensitive about this point. Hence they will try to be a "somebody" in the community in order to see their roles confirmed. In other words, they can be very competitive. Only when their positions are physically secure will they consider that the goal has been attained. If the psychic energy is obstructed, they can become hard-boiled, often out of sheer uncertainty, or can slide into a state of distraction or melancholy.

The fact that Capricorns are essentially dependent on the outside world and yet want to play an independent role in it, could be one reason why they find it so hard to show emotions. To do so, would be tantamount to revealing a chink in their armor— something they will do their best to prevent. And so, Capricorns may strike others as being cold, reserved and unapproachable.

What makes Capricorns really happy is being able to shape the world around them for their own comfort and safety. Frequently the other inhabitants of this world will be caught up in the plans they make, although most will find Capricorns inclined to preserve existing standards and traditions. This type of activity and, above all, the recognition that flows from it, feed self-importance. Appreciation will probably encourage them to continue working with energy and determination. If appreciation is withheld, Capricorns will try to gain it in all kinds of ways, since they look for it to confirm that they are on the right track. They may become very strict with themselves, and with others too, and may set themselves up as stern moralists. However, such extreme overcompensation will occur only if psychic energy is obstructed.

MOON IN CAPRICORN

The unconscious responses of people with Moon in Capricorn are typically earthlike: passive and with little initiative. The attitude is one of wait-and-see. Natives will be interested chiefly in real-life circumstances and situations, since they need security on the earth plane. Safe physical surroundings are one source of contentment; however, in addition to these, Moon in Capricorn seeks the security of a respected position.

Because these natives are to some extent under the influence of the cardinal cross, which tends to direct attention to our environment, and because in this case it is the unconscious mind (represented by the Moon) that is so directed, they will find themselves employing a passion for bringing order and control to things by accepting all the little responsibilities—even though it is not their direct intention to do so. What this does do is to give this Moon a clearcut role to play, which boosts a sense of security. If the role is questioned, these individuals can react violently from feelings of deep disturbance. Either they will reemphasize their own position and tighten control in an apparently cold and unfeeling way until others are left with no room to maneuver, or else they will pull out under the impression that nothing can be done with the situation, that they are worthless and useless—in a word they will become lonely and depressed.

The person with the Moon in Capricorn will not immediately show his hand in frankly emotional situations; an internal and external search for security make him want to create the best impression. Also, he will entertain strong feelings of responsibility for self and family, partly due to the craving for material security inherent in the element earth. An established position in society is something keenly desired. Nevertheless, because earth is so concrete, it is not particularly flexible, and this combined with the longing to look as good as possible in the eyes of the world means that Moon in Capricorn (to some extent this is also true of the Sun in Capricorn) will make heavy demands when it comes to keeping up appearances. His family may feel pressured by his regulations for its members, and much will be expected of the children. However, in getting the children to understand that there is work to be done in life, he may neglect the needs of the children themselves.

The individual with Moon in Capricorn has a typically conservative and practical response on all occasions, and constantly needs to know that he is a valued member of his community. Without this he can become withdrawn and inwardly frustrated but, seeing that Capricorn belongs to the cardinal cross, it is more likely that he will demonstrate his value to society at all costs.

MERCURY IN CAPRICORN

The thinking of someone with Mercury in Capricorn is concentrated on the practical and the concrete, which is why this placement of Mercury encourages logical patterns of thought. Everything must be arranged and analyzed in as clear, as concrete, and as realistic a manner as possible. What is more, the thinking is purposeful, not on its own account, but as a consequence of the fact that the native is inclined to use thinking to introduce order into the surroundings for the purpose of achieving material security. Therefore thoughts are always turning to matters concerned with the environment and the outside world at large in order to preserve things in as good a condition as possible. This demands long-term planning, and the individual is naturally purposeful. It needs no pointing out that the planning will go hand in hand with a disposition to structure and classify.

Down-to-earth, concrete, purposeful and plan-oriented thinking is an obvious characteristic of Mercury in Capricorn, and the need to set goals and to reach them through thick and thin (earth) often makes the individual with Mercury in Capricorn an intellectual achiever. The passion for gathering facts (Mercury) will find solid, practical expression here, and this makes a good basis for profound research. Since Mercury takes its time when in an earth sign, the motto will be "slow but sure."

Communication is not particularly lively, even though there is a need to keep in touch with the outside world. Contacts are more likely to be matter-of-fact. The earth influence tends to make the individual reserved in personal relationships, in spite of the fact that thanks to the cardinal cross Mercury is unable to do without them. This person prefers to join a circle of friends in which warm fellowship is combined with some shared interest that has a practical purpose.

Mercury here will talk quietly and calmly and will try to give good reasons for opinions. It is mainly factual and practical things which are of interest, and there is a tendency to stress the feasibility of projects; which means that Mercury will try to work out how to achieve the best results as economically as possible.

Should these people be denied the opportunity to think out ways and means of improving the outside world, or should they be unable to make an intellectual contribution toward turning the world into a safer place, they can overcompensate frustrations by adopting a very pessimistic attitude, by trying to forget the problem while spinning a web of secret thoughts, by engaging in long-term planning without letting anyone know, *or*—and given the presence of the cardinal cross influence this is the probable outcome—by working good and hard within the assigned limits (perhaps with some really painstaking mental effort) in the hope that hurt feelings can be shut out. Also, for fear of being unappreciated, they may lack the courage to leave the beaten track, remaining content with formal thinking that lacks originality, not to speak of being timid and hidebound. Given the right incentive, these people are usually capable of sober, logical thought with no frills but accompanied by deep concentration, and this can prove of great benefit to the outside world in which they are trying to establish themselves.

VENUS IN CAPRICORN

The human urge to find emotional and material security (Venus) expresses itself in an earth element way in Capricorn. Earth is concerned with matters that are practical and possessed of "genuine" value; hence Venus in this placement wants emotional security on the physical plane and a cosy niche in society.

Venus in Capricorn is not so eager to stretch out her hand to receive warmth as she is to dispense it. This does not mean that she has no need of warmth; quite the contrary. What it does mean is that whereas the element earth inclines her to be passive and restrained, the cardinal cross makes her want to be a "somebody" in the world and to stay in close contact with it. So there are problems. Venus needs the world so much that to avoid the tragedy of not being accepted by it she strives to create the best impression she can. Consequently, she will probably express herself in some concrete or practical fashion, by engaging in design work, by beautifying her surroundings and by seeking aesthetic certitude on the material plane. An industrious life style can also prove rewarding for the person with Venus in Capricorn, however, even though it may seem to have little to do with the emotions.

In a love relationship, Venus in Capricorn keeps her eyes on the other person, but the earth nature of the sign makes it difficult for her tongue to say all that is in her heart. She is often very faithful and will work hard to preserve a union that offers security.

The need for harmony and beauty is expressed in a very concrete manner, and the native may well take pains to build up a (permanently valuable) collection of paintings, antiques or the like. He or she may make a study of *objets d'art* or do something creative in the artistic field, and in that will resemble the individual who has Venus in Taurus. However, there is this difference, that with Venus in Capricorn the choice is largely determined by appreciation from others, while with Venus in Taurus the inner man decides.

If the energy of Venus in Capricorn is obstructed, anxiety can become the basis of her search for security, so that, for example, a potential partner is assessed on his ability to support her. Alternatively, she may become rather aloof, avoiding contacts with other people unless absolutely necessary. Yet solidly based security comes before everything else. She needs true love and true friendships; if these are denied her, she may overcompensate and try to prove her emotional worth to those whose esteem she would compel by working for them long and hard and with great dedication, or perhaps by acting in a standoffish manner to show that she is "above" such things. But, really, Venus in Capricorn makes the native long for a solid and reasonably prominent role to play in society and for well-deserved affection.

MARS IN CAPRICORN

The energy of Mars is given a clear direction when the planet is in Capricorn. Normally it is untamed, but here it is given physical reality and purpose. The cardinal cross forms a very suitable channel for the uninhibited planet. Mars and the cardinal cross both seek expression in the outside world, and, what with that and with the practical purposefulness of earth and of Capricorn in particular, Mars becomes a strong force in the psyche to enable the native to achieve whatever he sets out to do. Although the energy is canalized, it is not diminished. The Capricornian determination and insight into what can be done with matter enable very efficient use to be made of the Martian energy. The native can put in plenty of hard work without becoming distracted by anything foreign to the goal.

In spite of its controlled aggression when in Capricorn, Mars, in its capacity as the need to distinguish oneself from others, can adopt a very independent and self-assertive stance. The native's ambition may reveal itself externally (cardinal cross) on the physical plane (earth) as the struggle for a good social position. Along with this show of energy, Mars can exercise considerable self-discipline and perseverence in the pursuit of aims, and will not lose heart in the face of obstacles but will work with grim determination to clear them from the path.

Although Mars in Capricorn folks are so thoroughly individualistic, they do need others—as do those who have other planets in Capricorn in their charts. They need the to provide a background for their own activities.

The spirit of self-preservation in the native and a desire to prove the self manifest in an earth manner: he is always trying to create tangible security, while the cardinal cross influence encourages him to release inner tensions by making contacts with the outer world and by playing a definite part in it. Opposition can intensify ambition; excessively so in fact, so that either he wears himself out by doing too much or else spreads himself thin and wastes energy on matters of secondary importance.

Martian aggression is tempered in Capricorn, but can be very cold and calculating and very purposeful. However, Mars in Capricorn is a placement in which natives are fairly easygoing provided they are free to match themselves against the outside world.

JUPITER IN CAPRICORN

The need for spiritual and religious values is directed by Capricorn to things of practical and "real" worth. This often means that the native's faith rests on dogma and ritual—in other words, he can become an ultratraditionalist. Expansion and improvement are mainly sought on the material plane: the expansion of the personality from a material and a social point of view.

The person with this planetary position will be keen to prove himself, preferably in an organizing and controlling capacity that offers him (material) security. At the same time, any inner satisfaction has to be well and truly earned. Certainly, there will be ambition at times, especially when the natural psychic flow of the Jupiter energy is inhibited; but more often there is simply a need to be valued for his practical merits—particularly when at work.

Facts and events are usually looked at as realistically as possible and judged according to their practical value or meaning for the present or the future. The man or woman with Jupiter in Capricorn can do much to improve the material circumstances of self and others. Under the earth element influence he or she seldom neglects personal interests and, because of the presence of the cardinal cross, will seek some form of status in the community.

Like all the other planets, Jupiter when in Capricorn will try to make itself extra powerful if its energy is obstructed, even though, due to the earth element, it can have inward-looking tendencies which absorb part of the energy flow naturally. The reaction may be one of drawing attention to the native by "acting big," especially by passing critical comments on any little mistake made by others in the course of practical everyday living.

As already said, there is a solid basis for the native's spiritual and religious values, but it may also happen that, for Jupiter in Capricorn, material things become endowed with a spiritual value.

SATURN IN CAPRICORN

Saturn in Capricorn is in its own sign and is therefore able to express itself in its purest form. But Saturn, as the process of learning through suffering, will sometimes bring it about that the native's need to discover his own identity and worth penetrate consciousness in a painful manner. The sensitive point with Saturn in Capricorn is his role in society, and so he diligently works to secure it. Therefore, the native can appear to be ambitious, egotistic and very competitive; but that is only one of the overcompensations for his anxiety. What is central is his vulnerability over personal identity, over his actual role in life and his idea of what the latter ought to be. There may be a wide gap between the last two. Thus the individual may function well in the outside world and may enjoy a well-established position there, and yet feel very inadequate and very unsure of himself, with the result that, as a form of overcompensation, he will work hard to drown out the sound of the inner questioning voices. By so doing he can achieve a great deal, but it is a moot point whether or not he will take pleasure in his achievements; because of his sense of inadequacy, he will be fearful of losing the thing for which he so fretfully strives.

Once people with Saturn in Capricorn come to understand themselves and their weaknesses, they can work through the latter to arrive at a further development of the Sun—the ego. Of course, this process will be governed by the nature of Capricorn and will be influenced by the need for a sense of reality, the need to keep an eye on the concrete and practical, and the need to play a valued part responsibly and with perseverance. These individuals long to make something of themselves, and if hindered will insist even more strongly on their right to do so.

URANUS, NEPTUNE AND PLUTO IN CAPRICORN

The need to break the mold of form and to produce something new and original (Uranus), the need to refine form, to release it from its old attachments and to make it universal (Neptune), and the craving for power, confrontation and transcendence (Pluto), are expressed in Capricorn mainly in a social context, and in things to do with external concrete reality. And so Uranus tends to reshape things within the existing scheme and to replace outworn structures by new ones. Nevertheless, the originality implied by the planet is somewhat hampered by the fact that this sign is so strongly attached to forms and to the preservation of material security. However, there may be problems with authority: the native may think of new ways to challenge the powers that be.

Neptune in Capricorn will give a strange cast to the identity and authority principle, idealizing them, say, in a completely impractical manner. As much as Neptune might attempt to work in a practical way when in Capricorn, this is against its nature, because it is a vehicle for the imponderable and spiritual. The native may adopt a very idiosyncratic attitude toward everything material and possessed of fixed form or structure.

Pluto finds a good arena in Capricorn for power conflicts which have the aim of reforming social structures and of redistributing authority and so on.

All three planets have an influence to exert in the outside world, thanks to the practical nature of Capricorn; but much of what they will do lies well in the future.

Chapter Five

Planets in the Element Air

1. Mutable Air: Gemini

Sun in Gemini

The individual with the Sun in Gemini is naturally fitted to achieve self-realization by means of very lively thinking. The element air, taken by itself, tends to produce a fairly active mind, which certainly becomes no less animated when the mutable cross enters the picture. Consequently, the native can display considerable versatility, especially in the mental and intellectual sphere (air). Mutable thinking is mainly directed toward making connections, bringing about transitions and keeping interactions going; so that people with Sun in Gemini will come into their own in situations where they can open up lines of communication and handle and distribute a large quantity of things.

Because of a need for newness and change (the mutable cross), attention will be perpetually attracted by fresh theories and facts, etc. Geminis are endlessly inquisitive and will usually be well informed about whatever is going on.

A need to approach life with the mind, a facile manner of thinking and a craving for a constant supply of new impressions, often gives Geminis a certain superficiality. This does not worry them in the least, as they do not feel inclined to dwell on any one thing too long. New is attractive—but "ages" remarkably quickly. They like to defer serious study to a later date. The mutable cross faces both ways, both to the inner and to the outer worlds, but when the outgoing element air adds its infuence, the inner world often has to take second place. However, once the unconscious part of the mind breaks through (and for air that is the element water), the irrepressible curiosity of Gemini can turn its attention on all the strange and whimsical things they sense within themselves, and they will try to discover this presence in others too, sometimes to the verge of indiscretion.

The changeableness of Geminis make them appear as the bright butterfly of astrology, but this is not their own perception of themselves. Often they fail to work out the implications of what they have found, nor do they apply the facts discovered to themselves; but they can easily end up with a huge assemblage of data, all neatly pigeonholed and arranged, yet not particularly coherent. They like classifying. This stimulates thinking and gives some semblance of order—and order is needed sorely in view of the unceasing hunt for new things. There is some loose connection between the findings, but Geminis seldom arrive at making a proper synthesis—probably never even try to do so.

The need to keep moving in the mental sphere means that the Gemini native is soon hot on the trail of a new theory, which will be enthusiastically announced to friends and acquaintances; however, we need not be surprised if Gemini turns up next day with equal enthusiasm for a fresh, sometimes completely contradictory, theory. No time is given to reach a firm conclusion or to make a thorough investigation of everything met on the way.

Because Gemini individuals have so many things of which to take stock, they are likely to have a number of irons in the fire at once. Quick thinking contributes to this, and they are frequently quick and adroit in handling quite a variety of projects. The mental alacrity of the sign displays itself physically in a great liveliness of word and gesture. Only when energy is obstructed will they take refuge in overcompensation. Their minds can keep reaching after new things, regardless of whether material circumstances assist them or not. One possibility is that they will start fantasizing and perhaps telling falsehoods. Because the stimulus provided by a stream of new experiences is so necessary to the mind, they will invent them if necessary. Thanks to a great adaptability, they fit in easily with the outside world, and can even—in the event of any blockages—adjust the inner world to the given circumstances.

The speed and agility of Gemini natives, and the way in which their minds jump from one thing to another, can give others an impression of restlessness and nervousness—not entirely without good reason. But the question is not simply one of compelling them to "slow down," to become more settled, and so on, because that would go against Gemini's deepest nature. The Sun in this placement always prefers a more animated type of existence.

MOON IN GEMINI

An uncertain situation will elicit a quick mental reaction from the individual with the Moon in Gemini, without his being directly conscious of it. He tries to satisfy a need for security by taking brisk action, by using the mind and by connecting one thing with another: the mutable cross makes him keen to bring facts and opinions into line with one another whenever matters have become tense, while the element air encourages him to do so by means of communication and discussion. Like the person with Sun in Gemini, the Moon in Gemini individual likes to keep abreast of the latest news, and, in uncertain situations, will try to gain safety by supplying information in an impartial but lively manner, or by communicating in whatever way seems most appropriate. He can become a pacesetter, a thrower of parties, a smooth talker who easily persuades folks to get together, a reconciler of opinions.

If possible, the Moon in Gemini gives a greater need for change than does the Sun in Gemini, for in this way he soothes his unconscious mind. He is notable for his insatiable curiosity and will do anything to find out something new. Often he will look as if he is paying no attention, and yet not only will have taken in everything that has been said but will also have noticed a number of other items of interest which no one else has had time to observe. Concentration is certainly not his strong point, but he is capable of assimilating a great deal provided his curiosity is aroused and he does not become bored.

The unconscious emotional behavior is very intellectual in character, and the succession of his emotions cannot keep up with the procession of facts he passes in review. (The emotions associated with the Moon in an air sign must not be confused with the meaning we give to the word "feeling" when we use it in the sense of that function of consciousness to which we have assigned the element water.)

Generally speaking, the person with Moon in Gemini likes to have many contacts. The mutable cross craves contacts, and, when the element air joins it, it craves an abundance of contacts. The need for mental variety gives a desire for many and frequent encounters, with an accent on news gathering. Deep friendships are not so easily formed.

With an adaptation mechanism such as that of the mutable cross, which is geared to binding, loosing and integrating, someone who has Moon in Gemini will unconsciously feel happy going along with all sorts of changes, and will even have a positive need to undergo such changes frequently.

His neutrality (he does not stick to things long enough to form a fixed opinion about them) and his mental pliancy incline him to get inside someone else's skin so to speak, to live their life and think their thoughts, without, however, a genuine emotional involvement. A lively sense of mimicry is characteristic of people with Sun or Moon in this sign.

The conversational powers are good (just as with Sun in Gemini). The native's lively mind and versatility in making contacts can make him relate quite strongly to situations before he is aware of it. Because he needs to make sense of his emotional experiences, and to bring order into data and situations, the person with the Moon in Gemini is a planning and systems addict. Also he endeavors to express his knowledge in the clearest and simplest possible terms in order to share it with others. In fact, he has the makings of an excellent communicator.

If the energy imparted by the Moon in Gemini is obstructed, the mind may create a fantasy world in which there is nothing to distinguish between reality and delusion. Or perhaps the Gemini energy will assert itself in spite of everything and the individual will avidly set to work amassing facts and figures—at the risk of even more superficiality. Unsettled by the longing for change, nothing he starts is ever finished: he is content to be a "smatterer." In either case, the influence of the unconscious water element can break through from time to time, tempting him to heed gossips and sensation mongers.

To feel really at ease, the person with Moon in Gemini needs to employ his lively mind in the field of learning and in handling everyday events. He is well able to cope with difficult situations as long as his interest is retained.

MERCURY IN GEMINI

As a communicative, combinative and organizing psychic factor, Mercury is free to express itself in its own manner when in Gemini. Communication comes to the fore, and so does orderly thought; yet, this is subject to a need for change and variety, exactly as we find with the other planets in Gemini. The thinking process is therefore not so much concentrated as exploratory and versatile. Mercury reinforces the quick-working mind natural to Gemini. The active and orderly mental processes express themselves in a mental sign (an air sign) in a quick and adroit manner (air in combination with the mutable cross). Inquisitiveness is much in evidence and the power of absorbing information is also great. However, the facts, ideas, and opinions gleaned will not stay long in the memory; they will shortly be replaced by new facts and impressions, so the powers of retention are not always great.

Since it is concerned with the mental production of transitions, interactions and the like, associated with a need to integrate (the mutable cross influence), Mercury in Gemini may well express itself by all kinds of thought structures, communications systems, development programs and plans, etc. There is a need to handle facts and theories as logically as possible because, however much these natives know about these many subjects, they are always eager to clear the ground in order to start gathering more facts for some completely novel purpose.

The thought processes are quick and these natives talk hard to keep up with them. Sometimes they try to say so much all at once that they fail to make sense or stumble over their words. They will gesticulate or use mimicry in a lively fashion while speaking. They know how to communicate expressively, and, in fact, the communicative aspect is more important than the substance of what is communicated.

A nimble mind, inquisitiveness, a brisk approach and the practical inventiveness that flows from it make these people adroit and clever in many fields. With Mercury in Gemini, fluency of expression is good both in regard to the written and spoken word.

Constant alertness gives them a facility for jumping in with the most topical observations.

Mercury in Gemini needs to express those communicative, combining, and analyzing capacities using the mind as much and as quickly as possible. Obstructions cannot prevent this but can turn the active and restless energy inward. Then, all sorts of structures, categories and theories are newly spun for eventual expression in the outside world; but, when there is little opportunity to discuss ideas with others, Mercury in Gemini can get caught up in a web of abstract thinking that has no point of attachment to the world of concrete reality. Behavior of people like this sometimes degenerates into garrulousness. Tongues wag incessantly between bouts of silence. What is more, when the repressed energy bubbles out again, the influence of the unconscious water element can lead to irresponsible gossip.

People with Mercury in Gemini need change and interchange in the mental sphere, need to disseminate the collected facts, and so on. If prevented from satisfying these needs, they may try all the harder to do so in some way or other: perhaps by gathering scraps of worthless or cheaply sensational knowledge with which to "amaze" friends.

VENUS IN GEMINI

The emotional need for comfort and safety is rather restricted in scope in the sign Gemini; in this placement needs are expressed mainly mentally, so the person with Venus in Gemini like to have a partner with whom he or she can discuss all sorts of topics. The hand held out in the hope of receiving love is largely governed by the mind, and conscious communication takes precedence over the feelings. However, the Gemini craving for change makes the need for comfort and safety on the emotional plane changeable too, and this can work out in different ways in practice. Either Venus in Gemini has little idea of what is wanted on the emotional plane, or a variety is introduced into it by never staying too long with one partner. A permanent union must chiefly be based on friendship and the sharing of ideas, and is certainly not due to erotic attraction in the first instance.

Harmony and beauty are experienced in change as such. Therefore, fluency and harmony are prized both in art and in social contacts. The need for a warm, deep relationship (Venus) scarcely stands a chance in Gemini, which has so little inclination for anything deep. Sometimes there is a gnawing feeling arising from this without the native being able to pinpoint the trouble. An occasional irruption[19] (thanks to the regressive side of the mutable cross) of the inferior element water can obtrude powerful emotional needs, but Venus in Gemini is ill-equipped to handle them.

The variety provided by changing relationships and a multiplicity of friendships is highly valued. Admittedly, the person with Venus in Gemini desires to play an active part in society: he or she likes to talk, to exchange thoughts, to gather information and to satisfy a keen curiosity. But when certain relationships grow too intimate on the emotional level, the individual can become confused because the situation poses problems for a background mechanism which is of the mind rather than of the heart. Venus in Gemini often (unconsciously) prefers to avoid becoming too closely involved and treats more intimate contacts with a light and airy touch.

Obstructions or blocks in the personality can sometimes bring about a great exaggeration of the natural characteristics of Venus in Gemini. Social contacts are then sought more fervently than ever in the hope of overcoming the block by making up for missing quality with quantity. But the contacts which ought to bring emotional satisfaction often elicit no more than a mental response due to the native's defective attitude.

Whatever the case, Venus in Gemini offers the hand of love or friendship in a communicative and mentally lively manner and looks for a similar response. It would be futile to anticipate any expression of deep feelings in the first instance from this planetary position. These would arise in connection with other factors in the horoscope, or with the element water during its periodic incursions from the unconscious.

MARS IN GEMINI

An energetic influence such as that of Mars in a mutable air sign can hardly do other than engage in plenty of activity offering constant

---

[19]*Irruption* means to "burst in" versus the more common *eruption* ("to burst out"). Pub.

change. For Mars in Gemini, sitting still is awful: the native always has to have something to do, perferably serveral things at once—some of which will never be finished.

Because Mars also symbolizes the way in which we measure up to others, we would expect Mars to choose mental weapons in Gemini. The native will have no taste for physical violence but may use sharp remarks to demolish an opponent. He will tend to take the opposing point of view in any discussion; not because he really has another point of view (he has no time to formulate one), but because he enjoys the challenge of a verbal battle.

The activity pattern of Mars in Gemini is as variable as that of the other planets when in this sign. His dealings have a mental coloring; by which we mean that he will give a matter cursory consideration before moving into action. If obstructed, he will act unthinkingly and become liable to rush at things like a bull at a gate—with all the attendant consequences.

Since Gemini belongs to the mutable cross, the progressive direction of the psychic energy is now and then reversed, and the inferior element water floods in. Mars, in passing through a mental and mutable sign, is not equipped to cope with this inferior element. Although, to begin with, the native endeavors to treat the experience as impartially as he treats his normal experiences, because of its involuntary and incomprehensible nature and because of the need to communicate imparted by the mutable cross, he also wants to hear of similar states in others. This can sometimes lead to a hankering after the sensational and to somewhat unhealthy interests.

Mars accentuates the restlessness of Gemini. Even as a child the native needs constant attention as he wants to keep himself occupied and to have something new given to him to do all the time.

He develops his own personality most naturally along mental (air sign) lines, and has a penchant for repartee, entering into arguments in order to prove his ability in this direction. The instinct for self-preservation also manifests itself in a lively use of the mind; actually it looks as if this instinct is not particularly strong when Mars is in Gemini—a conclusion that appears to be borne out by the way in which the native keeps flitting from one novelty to another—but this is just the way in which he feels he can keep his head above water and preserve his identity. If he is hampered, his satirical wit may become even sharper.

JUPITER IN GEMINI

The inner need for expansion has fair scope for expression when Jupiter is in Gemini; for the "Twins" are not loathe to be on the move and are constantly going on to something new. Jupiter has another side to its nature and that is the need for having a broad and deep vision, and this side can suffer when the planet is in Gemini. Breadth of vision, which often goes hand in hand with the spiritual and religious needs of Jupiter, can produce a bottleneck here: the individual whose chart has Jupiter in Gemini will certainly endeavor to express this side of Jupiter in one way or another but, in may instances, seems to go no further than collecting an enormous number of facts of considerable interest without managing to synthesize them. The great attachment of Gemini to novelty and change makes it exceedingly difficult for the Jupiter factor to obtain the sort of synthesis it requires, in which things are experienced as a unity through their underlying connection.

Jupiter in Gemini will therefore often be characterized by a need to know much, to exchange a lot of information, to have many friends and acquaintances with whom to hold discussions; what is more, this Jupiter will often surprise auditors by the way in which unusual facts and figures are presented. And so, the deeper religious and spiritual needs represented by Jupiter will not in the first place be experienced inwardly when the planet is in Gemini, but will tend to find outward mental expression. The outcome may include clever thought constructions, systematic classifications of a wide variety of facts—or a fund of information that comes trippingly off the tongue. Expansiveness exists mainly on the mental, contactual and informational plane.

With the religious sense and the need for inner values so tied to logic (air) when Jupiter is in Gemini, the rational side of life tends to overlie the emotional side; but the inferior function that occasionally emerges via the mutable cross is liable to produce bursts of fanaticism. However, the cooler mental approach will quickly reassert itself.

The Jovian craving for inner values suffers violence here—it is unable to delve deep enough. Unsatisfactory though this may be, there is no help for it since Gemini simply does not offer enough depth for the planet's operations. Obstruction of the psychic energy only serves to reinforce the pattern, so that the native may develop many minor visions and isolated ideas with little feeling for wider issues.

SATURN IN GEMINI

As the weak spot in ego formation, Saturn when placed in Gemini may create problems for thinking and communicating (air). This does not mean that these natives are incapable of reflection—far from it. What it does mean is that thinking and communicating are felt to be somewhat unreliable and are therefore subject to overcompensation at times. Typical Gemini compensations follow the Saturnian anxiety and lack of self-confidence: everything is approached with the mind, sometimes too much so, to the exclusion of any emotional aspect. What is more, data are organized and categorized more readily than in many other planetary positions. Hence Saturn in Gemini is likely to gift these natives with a keen insight into systems theories and systems techniques. Yet, driven by the fear of failing to master a chosen subject, these natives will continue to immerse themselves in it. This is certainly true in economic matters, where there is a great accumulation of facts (or even an enslavement to facts) with no assurance that sufficient facts have been accumulated.

Communication is also under attack when Saturn is in Gemini. In other words, Saturn in this otherwise extremely talkative and socializing sign can make a taciturn person or a wallflower. However, that is merely one possibility; a nonstop chatterbox is the other extreme.

Life, with all its activities, is strictly regimented. Any divergence from the prescribed pattern is greeted with anxiety or a sense of insecurity, so that people with Saturn in Gemini can easily gain a reputation for inflexibility in thought and deed. In reality, this is no more than a mechanism for avoiding confrontation with the weak spot in the character. Change in the mode of life represents a source of trouble, and they prefer to accustom themselves to it gradually.

Saturn in Gemini is ideal for thorough, empirical research; for all phenomena are approached as systematically as possible—chiefly from a need to lay as firm a foundation as may be for the (supposedly) shaky thought processes.

Obstructions can give rise to various effects. Either these natives suffer from a compulsion to gather facts for the sake of it while clinging to familiar thought patterns for dear life, or else they experience a sense of uneasiness in the face of facts and knowledge, so that disturbances can occur in learning and communication—to the extent, perhaps, of producing stutterers. Essentially, such problems have to do with the psyche. Saturn will inevitably emphasize the mental and communicative aspect of Gemini, because this is where weakness and the root of anxiety lie—whether they are aware of it or not.

URANUS, NEPTUNE AND PLUTO IN GEMINI

The urge to destroy form and the craving for originality (Uranus), the need to refine and disassociate form and to make it universal (Neptune), and the need for power, confrontation and the transcendence of form (Pluto), take on a mental and lively coloring when these planets are in Gemini. The desire for fresh forms of communication, alternative approaches to facts, new ways of conveying information—but also the need for original thought—are characteristic of the placement of Uranus in Gemini.

Neptune's mode of expression is completely different. With Neptune, it is the need for a refinement of form and for the immaterial which find mental outlets. From a constructive point of view, this can imply research into invisible forces, into occultism and parapsychology. The least constructive expression is laziness of mind, impracticality, or paralysis of thought, due to the misty insubstantiality of Neptune wrapping itself around the native like a shroud. A feeble attempt is made to express Neptunian influence mentally, but the influence is one that easily eludes the grasp of the mind.

Pluto in Gemini encourages the native to go in search of hidden powers, but also to engage in power struggles on the mental plane. This need not be entirely bad, because clashes of opinion can produce new insights. The mind of the individual with Pluto in Gemini is much occupied with thoughts of reformation and restyling; this person may, in fact, be responsible for great revolutions in the world of thought, in the handling of facts and theories, etc.

Neptune and Pluto were in Gemini at the beginning of the twentieth century, and one need hardly mention how revolutionary this century has proved to be for those who have lived through it.

2. CARDINAL AIR: LIBRA

SUN IN LIBRA

Individuals with Sun in Libra prefer to follow a path that promises many contacts with the outside world and insures that they have a part to play in the community (the air element and the cardinal cross): they wish to be appreciated and to know their place. The element air is in itself strongly orientated toward the outer world; it gives a need for communication and exchange. Therefore, the cardinal cross, which is also outgoing, can only intensify the need. Librans are very dependent on the outer world, which is necessary to enable them to develop their conscious minds (something which is true of the natives of other Sun signs too, but seems to mean so much more to Librans), and so are particularly sensitive to whatever is happening around them. Disturbances in environment can have an upsetting effect on the development of their consciousness, which is why Librans are reputedly so peace loving. This peaceableness is not, however, based on some deep inner conviction but rather on an inwardly felt need to experience development of the hidden being. Therefore these individuals are so ready to compromise, so diplomatic and tactful, so much in favor of beauty and harmony: they need to be so for the sake of personal equanimity.

Because air is in this instance the conscious element, the element water, corresponding to the function of feeling, lies in the unconscious. In practice, this means that emotional questions can prove a sensitive matter for thoughtful Librans, and it is in emotional behavior that a lack of balance can reveal itself. Naturally, these natives will find it unpleasant when their emotional reactions run counter to striving for external balance and harmonious behavior. Hence it is not really accurate to say that Librans have an innate harmony: the truth is rather that they sense a continual disharmony and keep trying to change it to concord.

Doubting and the inability to choose, so characteristic of Librans, are easy to explain when viewed in this light. Choosing means saying "yes" to one thing while at the same time saying "no" to something else, and this is liable to upset that equilibrium about which Librans are so concerned. The constructive aspect of indecision, however, is that these people are well placed to see and understand the motives of both parties to a conflict; making it possible for them to take the part of a peacemaker and to reconcile opposing points of view. They are not so suited to the position of an ordinary judge, since verdicts imply making a clear-cut choice.

Seeing that the cardinal cross imparts a strong desire to play a valued role in the outside world, Librans tend to project themselves as amiable and lovable. Add to this the need to produce and preserve harmony in all things, and we get the type of people who put themselves out to be friendly and conciliatory, who love life and all its beauty and forms of expression, but who are, at the same time, rather vulnerable on these points. It is so essential for them to maintain the behavior described above that they are unable to develop further. Obstructions can lead to overcompensations such as impulsive searches for various enjoyments and for the "sunny side" of life—which may be symptomatic of a degree of laziness. When obstructed, these individuals may fall back into the type of behavior best described as "trimming one's sails to every wind," or else concentrate on social life at the expense of every other possibility. In the latter case, stress is laid on external appearances: outward harmony is achieved in order to disguise an inner lack of harmony.

Libra is an air sign and not an earth sign—therefore it does not have the same affinity as the latter with material things, and people with Sun in Libra can be successful at giving shape to things. This capacity is firstly employed in creating harmonious surroundings, in making a well-appointed home, say; but it may also find expression in working life so that contacts take place in a pleasant atmosphere. Indeed, it can enter into any sphere of activity where artistic insight would add a decorative touch. Actually, "decorative" is the operative word here, because decoration takes precedence over form (earth) for the native. If overstressed, decoration can become an obsession and can get in the way of comfort.

Not only is preserving a balance in the outer world very important, there is also the significant Libran tendency to see the self in one pan of the scales facing someone else in the other pan, so to speak. By looking into someone else as into a mirror, the natives can learn a great deal about themselves. Emotional bonds with others draw them closer to their own unconscious (consisting of the element of water, feeling), especially by means of the projection mechanism. The unconscious mind is quite inaccessible to Librans (at any rate in the first instance), because these natives' primary energy is progressive, that is to say moving away from the unconscious in the direction of a further differentiation of consciousness. But the stronger the conscious mind becomes, the more loudly will the unconscious mind clamor for attention at a certain moment. This means, for example, that Librans are particularly vulnerable to that crisis in middle age when the Moon and Saturn have moved one-and-a-half times around the natal chart[20] and the individual gradually veers from the external world and its values and gains an increasing appreciation of inner values. This is a difficult period for all cardinal sign natives, but especially for Librans, who are then confronted by their inferior element, water, in a way that can throw them uncomfortably off balance

MOON IN LIBRA

Even more than Sun sign Librans, those who have Moon in Libra need harmony and equilibrium in their immediate surroundings. Only in this way will they feel really comfortable and secure. They will be quick to exercise diplomacy in troubled situations and will aim at reconciling conflicts of opinion. Their own opinions will be carefully concealed, however, in the interest of restoring the status quo.

The adapability of those with Moon in Libra is considerable. A desire for a well-oiled social and business life is such that they do not feel happy when disputes and disorders arise and so will seek compromise in order to eliminate trouble. The need for social acceptance (cardinal cross plus element air) makes them eagerly affable but, in the first instance, there is little depth to the cordiality; they are unwilling to abandon private opinions.

New stimuli and new circumstances tend to be welcomed, and so people with Moon in Libra are well suited for activities in the field of communications: they are prepared to talk with anyone, pay attention to the smooth running of affairs, and keep a sharp lookout for latent tensions, which they will try to solve in passing. Yet, although they are "hail-fellow-well-met," they will not find it easy to enter into a deep relationship with one special individual. Making a choice of a thing or a person is a big problem to these natives; the preferred "choice" is to swim placidly with the tide. For this reason they are sometimes accused of being spineless. Nevertheless, in extreme cases, they understand quite clearly that desperate ills call for desperate remedies.

---

*See Hamaker-Zondag, K.M., *Astro-Psychology*, Samuel Weiser, Inc., York Beach, ME, USA, and The Aquarian Press, Wellingborough, UK, 1980, pp. 210-212.

If these natives have no opportunity for giving form and expression to the need for balance, harmony and social adaptability, various overcompensations can occur, especially as the Moon represents the behavior we adopt in order to feel at ease. In this instance, Moon sign Librans will do everything within their power to keep fulfilling this social role; even to the extent of offering services when there are absolutely no disputes to be settled or compromises to be reached.

When situations arise which require them to express personal opinions or to take firm stances, Moon sign Librans become anxious and can again overcompensate; if worst comes to worst, they will cease from their usual interventions and will wait to see what happens with an air of detachment, assuming a look of neutrality (but a really very superficial neutrality) as if matters had nothing to do with them.

Although Libra is an air sign and not an earth sign, and therefore not directly involved with the material world, the form-giving properties of the Moon do reveal themselves in these natives, especially in the social sphere. They know how to bring harmony into their home and place of work or anywhere else where people gather, and can employ their decorative abilities in other fields as well. It is not so important that the forms fit (as it would be if an earth sign were involved), as it is that the ensemble is redolent of harmony and taste and capable of exercising a pleasant influence on the contactual sphere. In overcompensation a certain luxuriousness and exactingness can make their appearance. Much will then be made of outward show instead of real contacts.

People with Moon in Libra have difficulty forming their own opinions and are therefore easily influenced. When considered with their weaker side, the element water, this characteristic makes them attach great importance to emotional relationships (here the role of the "other" comes in); also it makes them very receptive and teachable on account of their inner vacillation. There is a danger for them of being rebuffed when they enter into certain relationships on the basis of their emotions. Perhaps they continue to cling to someone with whom they no longer have anything in common, simply because to let them go would destroy their peace of mind. Another danger is that of allowing themselves to be carried away by all sorts of things in which they have no genuine interest. Should the inferior element (water) come to the surface (incidentally, this may take a long time to happen), they may become involved in grand confrontations through riding emotional hobbyhorses which, under the influence of the element air, they would never have ventured to mount. This state of affairs can prove upsetting both internally and externally. However, people with Moon in Libra would not run true to type if they did not eventually revert to their friendly and conciliatory mode of behavior, for this is what gives them the greatest sense of comfort.

MERCURY IN LIBRA

The thought processes of people with Mercury in Libra are primarily oriented toward imparting facts and figures (air) in such a way that those around can learn something of them (cardinal cross) and that, by doing so, a recognized role can be played in the community (again: cardinal cross). In practice, this is equivalent to thinking that is much concerned with social and business life, especially where there is a question of restoring harmony to the latter or of reaching compromises. These natives have outstanding abilities for combining the ascertained facts into an objective whole (air), but they have much more difficulty in forming personal opinions in regard to this whole. Choices will be "not to choose" but to systematically endeavor to steer a middle course. In practice, this means they will not "dig too deep" but will try to preserve a strict neutrality.

These natives use their experiences to achieve inner balance as far as possible—or to restore the balance when it has been disturbed. The analysis of situations, events, the environment, other people, and last but not least, themselves, serves the purpose of the function which Mercury in Libra would perform in society as a whole (cardinal cross influence).

The manner of conversing is amiable and quite engaging. Mercury in Libra chooses words carefully, doing their best to make themselves clear, not so much for the sake of concreteness as for the sake of not giving unnecessary offense. Difficult situations are solved (or rather smoothed over) in a friendly way, but there is seldom any real confrontation or in-depth discussion involved. Thses natives would find this far too disturbing to personal thought patterns and to their chosen way of handling contacts.

Mercury in Libra can induce considerable vacillation when it comes to making a choice, being easily influenced and will, for example, look to the partner for guidance and permission when a decision has to be taken. Where there are obstructions, natives can overcompensate in various ways. Doubt and indecision can be aggravated, but it is also possible that the treatment of others can go from friendly to fulsome, even when speaking to someone they dislike. Eventually all sorts of problems and conflicts are unveiled: social behavior gradually becomes more difficult until there is an outburst, the causes of which must be sought in the past. In general, however, these natives like to respond in a very optimistic and positive manner toward others. By doing so, they hope to sweeten any potentially sharp exchange and preserve the spirit of harmony.

VENUS IN LIBRA

A psychic influence such as that of Venus in a sign so strongly orientated toward the bringing or preserving of beauty and harmony is bound to find powerful expression. Since Venus in Libra has a great need for material, and even more for emotional, security, the planet will express itself by bringing as much harmony as possible to social behavior. In its capacity as the hand we extend to others, Venus in Libra will come across as warm, friendly, winning and agreeable, and this is how we may expect someone with that placement to behave.

In order to restore equilibrium and to unite opposites, these natives like to encourage amicable settlements of differences by indicating, in as friendly a way as possible, any points of agreement. Even in love, Venus in Libra acts in this fashion. Everything is weighed against everything else because Libra is an air sign and approaches matters through the mind—thinking being the primary function. Any difficulties with a partner will be solved by Venus in Libra with as much give-and-take as possible. Venus is prepared to climb down a long way, convinced that certain extreme character traits in both partners have to be moderated and that life can be lived without too much tension. A consequence can be the attaching of undue importance to external appearances, especially when there are obstructions to the flow of psychic energy. Venus in Libra natives will not readily desert a partner, and they prefer to remain on good terms with former lovers, even at the cost of some inner distress.

Venus in Libra may cultivate deeper contacts with considerable caution because the element water (feeling) is the inferior function here. But if ever this element breaks through (especially in a crisis) bringing the source of the native's uncertainty to the surface, he or she can make very heavy demands in a relationship for a while, and will forget about external affairs and circumstances. Nevertheless, the most likely result will be that the more extrovert side of Venus will receive extra emphasis when there are any obstructions, so that stress is laid on the part played in the outside world, on a show of friendliness, on flirting and on maintaining contacts on a superficial level. Inwardly, however, Venus will always have a great need for many friends and acquaintances, a warm relationship or union which is socially acceptable, and balance and harmony in the spiritual and material environment insofar as it can be experienced: all this because the harmony within is so precarious.

MARS IN LIBRA

Mars, as the innate drive to dissociate oneself from others, has problems in Libra, which is so dependent on others and attaches so much importance to cooperation and harmony in the environment. There is therefore something contradictory about this placement of Mars. On the one hand, there is a Libran background of harmonious and collaborating behavior, while on the other, there is the Martian reluctance to fit so snugly into society and the environment. Therefore, roughly speaking, we find two diverse energies in Mars in Libra.

For one thing, there is a strong urge to enter actively and energetically into social life, to make contact with and to work with others, to engage in all sorts of community activities and so on; and, for another thing, the individualistic nature of Mars can lead to the native to vie for position in any team joined. Nevertheless, Libra is a sign in which the self needs to see its image reflected in others (by projection). This means that Mars in this sign will let the native go a long way with others before an opportunity occurs to show its individualism. Even when the competitive spirit does raise its head, the rivalry can be friendly, since Mars is not so grimly determined in this placement: the other fellow's efforts will act as a stimulus to his own. But where the psychic energy is obstructed, there can be some pretty fierce reactions.

Because Libra is indecisive, these natives' energy may not be employed particularly purposively; they may, indeed, seem lacking in willpower. However, when they find themselves in stimulating circumstances—for example, where co-workers are all doing their best or where the boss is wielding a big stick—they can move mountains.

People who have Mars in a cardinal sign like to establish themselves in the world and to count for something in it; but when the cardinal sign is also an air sign this external role will also have to be involved with thought and communication. When in any of the air signs, Mars loves debates; in Libra, which is so dependent for growth on harmony in the surroundings and on relationships with others, this tendency is less easy to express—Libra inhibits Mars from pushing things to extremes. There is one thing, however, which can rouse the martian ire and that is injustice. Mars in Libra is always ready to take up arms against anything that would destroy harmony and will try to redress every form of wrong or unfairness, though not always with much tact. Here we stumble upon the singular duality of Mars in Libra. For while Mars here would make an excellent justice of the peace or a protester against anything that is antisocial, it can work for social harmony in a competitive spirit and with a sense of its own importance. Obstructions of the psychic energy can intensify these two types of behavior, and all kinds of overcompensation can arise out of the dualism: utter slackness, love of ease, a craving for luxury and indecision (when the energy is expanded on the preservation of a feigned balance or a feigned harmony), to the waging of war on injustice. Although ready to compromise to some extent, all that this amounts to is that the native is seeking an outlet for feelings of self-importance on the social plane (or in any person-to-person relationships) even while "doing good" by redressing the balance wherever possible.

JUPITER IN LIBRA

Jupiter in a cardinal sign will be very outward-looking, especially on the social and communicative plane (the element air). The need for every form of expansion and widening of the horizon manifests itself in the desire for many contacts, which need not go very deep initially. When Libra is the cardinal sign in question, balance is what is sought in the contacts rather than depth or instructiveness. The sense of justice is very strong with Jupiter in Libra; also the Libran need for harmony and beauty affects the way in which Jupiter handles expansion and improvement. The natives are fairly vulnerable on this point of justice and injustice. The problem is that when they decide to assist one party they realize they cannot help the other party, and this makes them wonder whether or not they made the right decision: even after weighing the pros and cons, they have great difficulty in making a choice.

The spiritual and religious needs of individuals with Jupiter in Libra are mainly based on the desire to join others in a common cause. Their faith will encourage them to work for peace. However, this faith is not necessarily a faith in God: faith in the benefits to be derived from certain social improvements can also serve as a strong incentive.

The expansiveness of Jupiter in Libra is found chiefly in the area of contacts and in the creating of balance. Therefore the number of relationships formed is very important to these natives, since inner growth in every direction can depend on the experience gained from their many mental contacts. They are likely to see themselves reflected in their surroundings and in the mutual reactions of their surroundings and themselves. So among the possibilities open are an increase in inner maturity and the opportunity to see facts in a wider context after entering into communication (air) with the outer world, and by playing an active part in it (cardinal cross).

SATURN IN LIBRA

Peace and harmony and relaxed contacts with others are sensitive issues for those who have Saturn in Libra. For that reason they are often nervous about confrontations and have an exaggerated need for harmonious surroundings. However, this Saturnian nature is so quick to become dependent on its environment that it is usually only after a number of painful experiences that they learn the importance of looking within and of putting the "inner man" under the magnifying glass. For although Libra, as both an air and a cardinal sign, is oriented toward the outside world, Saturn is just as surely orientated toward the inside world—where it engages in uncovering the kernel of the individuality.

Anxieties and inhibitions can indicate the indispensability of building an inner identity before trying to play a part in the outer world—hard though the effort may be when Saturn is in Libra. With this placement, consciousness is formed in a mental way (thanks to the element air), and it is natural for these natives to share in the activities going on around them for the sake of being accepted. In fact, because they are so sensitive on this point, they will often go out of their way to win acceptance, elbowing into the foreground and continually alienating themselves from that to which they unconsciously attach the most value: a harmonious social life.

Since they are so devoted to balance and harmony on the social and contactual plane, people with Saturn in Libra will pick and choose words with care. A sense of obligation and responsibility in a relationship and in regard to others is considerable, and sometimes this takes away some of the joy of life. The sense of justice is also well developed for this planetary influence creates such a sense of responsibility when posited in the sign that weighs right and wrong. Nevertheless, difficulty in choosing also comes into the picture here, so that it is safe to assume that any choice made will be based on a great deal of factual information and on a reasoned consideration of the data collected.

When in Libra, the "planet of learning through pain" has more than the usual need to live in pleasant surroundings among congenial companions. If there are difficulties in the path leading to these objectives, natives will be incited by the Saturnian influence to try and manipulate circumstances so as to surround themselves with harmony and beauty—evidently taking the line of least resistance— before exploring inner potential. Concentrating on externals brings neither lasting peace nor satisfaction—it is only a stay of execution. Breaking the mental form of a relationship, contact by confronta- tion, or talking a thing through is hard for people with this position of Saturn. Nevertheless, if progress is made thus far, these social experiences will enable the natives to learn about personal anxieties, faults and problems. The insight obtained into what they do and don't do will help them to shape up better than before. As a bonus, they will be more capable of bringing harmony and beauty into the environment without being so dependent on the latter. All the same, the road is a hard one, because involvement with the outer world is so essential to those with Saturn in Libra.

URANUS, NEPTUNE AND PLUTO IN LIBRA

The tendency to break the mold of form and to seek originality (Uranus), the need to refine form, to dissociate it and to make it universal (Neptune), and the need for power, confrontation and transcendence (Pluto), have a mental and communicative cast when in Libra and work strongly in the external world (due to the combination of the element air and the cardinal cross). When

Uranus entered Libra and moved through it from 1969 through 1974, it became clear that old forms of society and community action had undergone a radical change. This change was a long time coming and, having come, was irreversible. New aesthetic values and concepts took the field and alternative forms of balance and harmony were sought. Children with this placement of Uranus grew up in a time which bore traces of this development and they were destined to continue it.

The pathway for the development had already been prepared by Neptune on its transit through this sign from 1943 through 1957. Ideas concerning the structure of society became vague. There was an obvious need for idealistic relationships to replace the old style relationships to a large extent. The hippies and the flower-power people belonged to the generation which had Neptune in Libra, and they confronted the world with their revolutionary notions of how people should live together—setting up communes and so on. Now that Pluto has been having its long sojourn in Libra we see yet another break with old patterns. Children with this placement will pay scant heed to the picture handed down by society of what social life ought to be like. This is a difficult period for an influence such as that of Libra, which is directed toward achieving harmony. Pluto strips the familiar friendly forms of their frills and exposes what lies below the surface—which is more than we sometimes think. The time of Pluto in Libra is the time of confrontation in interpersonal contacts, and this understandably creates problems. The accompanying changes can, at best, wipe society's slate clean and give it a fresh start. Those who have Pluto in this position will be caught up in the trend and many will, either consciously or unconsciously, attempt to build some new social structure.

3. FIXED AIR: AQUARIUS

SUN IN AQUARIUS

As with all the air signs, the conscious attitude here is governed by the mind. The world is approached logically, or at least by the use of reason, and is subjected to analysis. Facts are placed in a theoretical connection, relationships are seen between the discovered patterns and interactions, and so forth. Yet because the fixed cross is dominant, the conscious mental attitude cannot function without certain emotional impulses. In fact, when the regressive movement of the Aquarian psyche brings certain emotional contents to the surface (and emotional water is the inferior element here!), it determines the native's further conscious outlook and behavior, even though, by virtue of its being inferior, the emotional content may seem foreign to the conscious mind of an Aquarian. The native never theorizes wildly, but is always factual in his thinking even though, to a degree, he identifies emotionally with the subject engaging his attention. Thanks to the influence of the fixed cross, he can remain preoccupied for a long time with his chosen theme. The same permanence of attachment characterizes his relationships with others: it is difficult to break away from them. Once the mind falls under the spell of the feelings arising from the inferior function, he loses his normally clear-sighted approach for the time being.

For a thought oriented Aquarian, the emotional side of life often appears rather threatening because it presents experiences which cannot be put into words or sentences; if, therefore, there is any obstruction of the psychic energy, he can fall into either of two extremes of behavior. One possibility is a capriciousness of reaction to spontaneous, unconscious impulses, so that behavior becomes very erratic and there is no means of knowing what his next move will be. It is not altogether correct, as is often done, to ascribe this to a passion for liberty and reform. What is really going on is that he is trying to release himself from the grip of his own unconscious—a difficult task on account of the influence of the fixed cross. Not that the person with the Sun in Aquarius is incapable of being progressive or reformist—he often is so. However, he does not always understand his own motives very clearly since they may be derived from an internal conflict with his inferior element, to which he may give either a positive or a negative shape.

Another form of behavior in which the native may take refuge when things get too much for him is to reinforce his conscious function and to suppress feelings and emotions. The result is a sterile attitude in which the native uses thinking to prove himself; an attitude that can persist for a long time because it seems so easy to the conscious mind. However, because by adopting this attitude the conscious mind severs relations with the unconscious mind, there is nothing to call the conscious mind to order when it gets out of line. Hence consciousness can sometimes grow out of all proportion. Apparently, its position in the life of the native is unassailable, but touch it on a vulnerable spot and you will find it has little strength or depth. Incidentally, this explains why the usually unflappable Aquarian can fly into a panic in an unexpected emotional situation. But this is something he prefers not to have mentioned.

The inward flowing energy of the fixed cross inclines people with the Sun in Aquarius to ruminate over what happens. Experiences are absorbed for mental processing, and they continue to activate the emotions until they have been assimilated. Thus the "airiness" of the element air has to a great extent disappeared in the fixed sign Aquarius to make way for a greater tenacity; which is why Aquarians cling to certain ideas and will not abandon them unless they have an inner conviction that the alternative is better.

Since the fixed cross relays emotional impulses to the conscious mind and, in doing so, can undermine it, these natives will seek to reassure themselves in some way or another; if possible, by taking advantage of the communicative abilities of air to make intellectual contact with others, preferably with those having the same tastes and views. When overcompensation strengthens the conscious function, we may find that Aquarians become fellow travelers in a group for the sake of certain ideas advocated by the group.

Due to the internal confrontation continually going on inside, Aquarians make good psychologists because they have a feeling for what goes on inside other people too. The inferior function, feeling, paired with their flair for communication (air) certainly help them in this direction. By the same token, they are strongly in favor of liberty and equality for all. They are acutely aware of the fact that each one of us has human failings and problems, and that worldly status does nothing to change this. Fixed cross individuals have little respect for outward show that does not serve some inner purpose. Aquarians, in particular, may give the impression of being rebels against authority and social norms. This is a consequence of a sense of the inner equality of all people and of their own internal struggles, in which the 'authority' of the conscious mind is constantly being undermined by incomprehensible emotions belonging to the unconscious. For the natives themselves such internal struggles are very necessary if they are to avoid overcompensating as described above.

The tension between thinking and feeling can lead to wholly original and inventive ideas. Reformation, not to mention revolution, is second nature to Aquarians, whether their particular field of interest be sociology, communications, technological research or science.

If the natives' energy is obstructed, we may expect to see—in addition to the possibilities mentioned above—a number of different attitudes, from iconoclastic tendencies born of anarchism to the desire to construct something more human after a period of decay. The heart of the matter with Aquarians is the need to be able to express the inner conflict between (unconscious) feeling and (conscious) thinking—a conflict perpetuated by the fixed cross—both within and outside themselves. Where there are tensions, this can do much harm socially, but on the other hand it can help to bring about long overdue changes.

MOON IN AQUARIUS

When people who have Moon in Aquarius feel insecure, they put on their thinking caps so as to get things in some sort of order, preferably to repress any disruptive feelings, and to analyze matters as calmly and as collectedly as possible. The fixed cross influence insures that the analysis is deep and thorough. However, all this mental activity provokes repressed feelings, and so these natives find themselves perpetually on the horns of a dilemma. They have to abandon meticulous reasonings and insights because they are emotionally unsettled. The uncertainty makes them think things over anew, and eventually they become trapped in a vicious circle. Like those with Sun in Aquarius, these natives would gladly deny the unconscious function of feeling and would rely wholly on mental activities, but this is not possible with an emotional factor like the Moon. Sooner or later, Moon sign Aquarians will be confronted again by the rejected emotions.

Individuals with Moon in Aquarius have a distinct need for liberty and fraternity, more distinctly so than has the Sun sign Aquarian. The need is certainly present in the latter, but here it is more compelling: natives have an absolute necessity to be free and independent yet not too different from others, because only then can they feel at ease. They make their bid for independence fairly early in life but do not remain "loners." As members of the communicative air signs, and just like their Sun sign brothers, they will seek confirmation of their thoughts by keeping in touch with others; but, with the lunar influence, there has to be a sense of security, a security that these natives prefer to find in the company of like-minded people or a group. The need for such company is paramount;

sometimes they travel with their ideas from group to group without falling in line with the tenets of any.

Moon sign Aquarians are very sensitive to all sorts of theories and ideas and can therefore be either very much in favor of or very much opposed to certain extreme views. If we take into consideration this need for their own free development, we shall be able to appreciate that they are likely to feel the greatest affinity for unconventional systems and philosophies; therefore, like Sun sign Aquarians they have a revolutionary streak in their makeup. Hard though it may be for the Sun Aquarian to knuckle under to authority, it is even harder for Moon sign Aquarians to do so, since they have to decide about good and evil for themselves, or so they imagine (the fixed cross conforms only with itself!).

The unconscious feeling function and a need for a logical approach can make them want to reshape society. The unconscious emotions can catch them off-guard, so that they feel for the sufferings of others and protest against "illogical" and unreasonable social structures which give insufficient guarantees for individual freedom and opportunity. In fact, they may become champions of social reform. Often their approach to such problems will be constructive; but, if opposed, it may become destructive and violent.

With Moon in Aquarius, natives can get entangled in emotional situations—for example, by falling for someone mistaken for the "real McCoy." Unconscious emotional life sweeps them off their feet so suddenly that they are parted from rational moorings. They may then give the impression of being very emotional, although this is not the true nature. Of course, they are not without feelings, but they have absolutely no control over emotional processes, which can turn them upside down. They, however, will just as quickly endeavor to scramble back into a position from which they can make a more "satisfactory" mental evaluation of events.

When all is said and done, Moon sign Aquarians need to approach the world as logically and as systematically as possible; however, owing to the fixed cross influence, they do not escape from emotional challenges. Here lies the source of their unpredictable behavior, but here also lies the source of creativity.

MERCURY IN AQUARIUS

Mentally alert Mercury is "at home" in the air sign Aquarius. It can give expression to the need for thinking, analyzing and arranging in a logical and systematic manner in keeping with its influence on human thought life. Therefore, people with Mercury in Aquarius will want to indulge in all kinds of theories, ideas and so on, which, incidentally, need not be particularly down to earth. The facts they encounter in everyday life are marshalled in a logical, perspicuous manner and worked up into a systematic whole. On account of the fixed cross influence, Mercurian minds will have to cope with various illogical impulses beyond the pale of reason, originating from the inferior element, water. And so, from time to time, definite emotional components enter into the thinking, with one of two results. Either they pass themselves off as very objective but are really extremely subjective, or else they experience extra depth in their thinking and therefore can devote themselves with heart and soul to anything with which they indentify emotionally. Of course, they are well able to approach the world with a show of reason; explaining *why* they are so busiliy engaged, and *why* work is so "important." However, if we really want to know just why they do what they do, we have to brush aside all those spurious reasons to discover the answer in their unconscious emotions. People with Mercury in Aquarius are very sensitive to those forms of "manipulation" which play on their feelings.

Thinking is often profound (fixed cross), and because of a continual need to understand things (especially the internal conflict of which they are ever aware), Aquarius Mercury finds "man" and "nature" extremely fascinating. On turning attention to any area of tension, they can often help people to a better understanding, since they appreciate the fact that each of us has problems. The Aquarian mind favors equality, and this predilection is very marked when Mercury is in this sign. Hence a need to think, to exchange views and to make contact is not confined to a single individual; they like to deal with numerous people and situations, to see what needs to be done and to make appropriate plans. Concern is not so much to overthrow any of the powers that be as to incorporate men and events in theoretical structures.

Although individuals with Mercury in Aquarius give plenty of evidence of clear thinking, they are surprisingly difficult to influence on certain ideas and topics. Whereas they will keep an open mind on most things, the fixed cross influence can keep the mind completely closed on some particular issue. No one can change them; only they themselves can alter personal opinions. In fact, the fixed cross acts as a definite curb on the mutability and "airiness" of Mercury, even though it is here in an air sign. Natives keep their eyes and ears open for other people's opinions and theories, however, and they are not set to defend a given idea come what may; if they see for themselves that an alternative idea is better, they will go over to it or will try to integrate it into personal existing thought patterns. To sum up this point then, the natives do have a certain fixity of thought and concept but are prepared to consider new or, at least, alternative trends which others might be ignoring. In this way they develop originality.

Because the implications of old, traditional standards and values are often fully worked out, these people will quickly tire of them. They are happier when thinking about something in which they have a chance to be creative, and to which they can make personal contributions. This may mean that they are decidedly unconventional on certain points. If the psychic energy is obstructed, originality and unconventionality can become eccentricity and exhibitionism. But, whatever the case, the energy will find some form of expression.

VENUS IN AQUARIUS

The need for emotional and material comfort and safety is expressed in Aquarius primarily in a mental way. Mental communication and exchange are central in the striving for certainty. When Venus in Aquarius extends the hand of friendship, it is done more with the mind than with the heart. A cheering word or a good chat strike these people as being more effective than a consoling hug. Yet they will have a great need for the latter whenever the influence of the inferior element, water, manifests itself, even though they instinctively rationalize and assimilate those feelings that assail them during unguarded moments. In company, they will be affable, communicative, comradely and, in general, easy to talk to. On a more intimate level, they may prefer to admire the partner for her or his mind and the partner will have to overcome a reluctance to give themselves to a mate completely.

The search for harmony is governed by the air (thinking) function, so beauty in the arts and aesthetic values in social behavior are approached from a logical point of view if possible. However, the fixed cross can limit the flexibility of social and business life, since Venus in Aquarius will often stick resolutely to personal opinions. And when the inferior element, water, enters the scene, these individuals may keep looking for emotional security in relationships that have long lost real meaning; nevertheless, if only they can find in it something to satisfy the mind, they will continue to cling to it. The fixed cross is also responsible for the fact that Venus in Aquarius often expects a lot of the partner. On the one hand there has to be good mental rapport and everything has to be discussed in as balanced (mental) a manner as possible, so that the two partners have to be well matched as regards what they contribute to the relationship. On the other hand, the mate must be able to handle the force of the element water, which Venus in Aquarius itself hardly understands, and the partner must be capable of sustaining an intense emotional union under the cooler mental union.

Because Venus in Aquarius can be apprehensive over the feelings which rise up inside, people with this placement may resist forming too strong an emotional union. They will enjoy casual flirtations, say, and have many superficial friendships for which others may envy them, but will remain unsatisfied deep down. Sooner or later the influence of the fixed cross will persuade them to listen to the inner voice. Even without going so far as to play coquette, Venus in this sign will want to seek a degree of emotional security by communicating with others. Venus here is set on a companionable meeting of like minds. When frustrated, Venus may cultivate an independent and cerebral approach, but deep within there is a gnawing desire to give emotions a chance via the fixed cross. And so an inhibited Venus in Aquarius can sometimes lose its mental bearings and can sojourn in higher spheres without taking any further interest in down-to-earth reality or logic. The native must give free rein both to the mental processes and to the occasionally violent emotional aspect in order to be happy.

MARS IN AQUARIUS

The innate drive to break free and to distinguish oneself from others finds mental expression in this air sign, so that these natives, in common with those who have Mars in the other air signs, are sharp debaters and quick at repartee. Since the fixed cross controls their psychic energy, they can also prove very loyal to a particular vision and will defend it for a long time. Sometimes they will stick to their guns against better judgment from a wish to be mentally provocative. More than anything else, this is an expression of the aggressive side of an instinct for self-preservation.

The executive power and the energy of Mars in Aquarius are considerable provided one requirement is met: the natives must be able to identify with whatever they are doing. Then they will be able to move mountains. Otherwise they find it hard to get down to work. Through the fixed cross effect they are confronted with the element of feeling (water) and this will periodically upset their conscious mental approach to what they do and will now and then fill their minds with motivation straight from the unconscious. These natives will advance a thousand and one reasons explaining why they behaved in exactly the way they did, but in many instances these reasons will have occurred to them in retrospect.

Mars prompts individuals to prove themselves. Because Mars is mentally alert and quick to see connections and theoretical implications, these natives will often respond with pointed remarks which may not be to everybody's liking. On the other hand, they will probably be able to state the case for certain sections of society clearly and sometimes challengingly and, if convinced of being right, will not be afraid to join issue with the establishment or (more abstractly) with traditional values and mores. These natives are therefore well placed to bestow energy intelligently on all sorts of humanitarian and reform projects provided they are attractive. Although Aquarius, like the other air signs, tends to promote the powers of thought, this is no guarantee of a sense of realism. The person with Mars in Aquarius is quite likely to be filled with enthusiasm for impractical notions, for Utopian plans and so on, and on occasion will want, with or without the backing of some group, to "reform" or change existing conditions with which little is wrong.

The influence of Mars is exerted not only on the outside but also on the inner person, where it may act independently from the inferior element (water) so undermining to the native's self-confidence. Such alienation from something basic to the nature can make one cold and merciless, and completely absorbed in isolated ideals, ideals that can be ruthlessly promoted without regard for anyone else's point of view. However, the element water will continue to complicate the issue until either the native's behavior spirals increasingly into the cerebral and impersonal, or else reaches a breakthrough point into a place where one can make a positive and humane contribution to society—and this may be done provided one can "find oneself" as a result, and can be free to express individuality in some form or other. Insights gained early on from inner conflicts via the fixed conflicts via the fixed cross may help later in life.

To put it in a nutshell, the person with Mars in Aquarius can sometimes overcompensate because the mind is the instrument mainly used to reassure himself. If unsuccessful, he can lay even greater emphasis on this "instrument" becoming totally alienated from himself or until, owing to some crisis, he has found another way (also mental) of proving himself.

JUPITER IN AQUARIUS

Spiritual and religious values spring from within when Jupiter is in Aquarius (a fixed sign), but must also comply with the laws of logic (Aquarius being also an air sign). Because they come from within, the inwardly hidden water element has a part to play in them. People with Jupiter in Aquarius feel that certain values are important and expound on them in a clear and rational manner. Jovian expansiveness is governed both by the mind and by the unconscious emotions. This means that Jupiter will spread its expansive and improving influence in areas favored by the natives (due to an emotional identification with those areas), especially when the natives can persuade themselves and others that such action is both reasonable and acceptable. Other people are important to them only insofar as they can be easily convinced by them; they themselves are not open to being convinced. Jupiter has the fixed cross outlook here, which means in the first instance, only the natives' inner feelings are important to them and whatever the world may think of them is not.

Facts and events are seen mainly in a wide social setting. Social activities (regardless of their scale) are significant to those belonging to the air sign Aquarius because they find it easy to express themselves this way (air being the element of communication). Hence Jupiter in an air sign will inject some of its energy into the social field—after coming from within the individual due to the influence of the fixed cross. Because the initial motivation is so intensely personal, there can be a certain compulsiveness about the improving and expansive activities, as the inferior element of feeling, water, interferes with the exercise of reason.

The fixed cross, which is so obsessed with inner values, makes it hard to influence anyone who has Jupiter in Aquarius. It is not the person who utters an opinion who matters to this Jupiter, but the sense or otherwise of the opinion itself. Consequently, the native is free and unfettered in the development of personal activities; something which could certainly not be said of everyone. Therefore, Jupiter here can accomplish much that others would never think of attempting. The danger is that this Jupiter can become so self-opinionated that nothing and nobody can influence the individual, so a great deal of useful energy can be wasted.

SATURN IN AQUARIUS

Although Saturn is naturally the night ruler of Aquarius and ought to be compatible with this sign (which is partly true), this placement is not without its problems for the inner man. Even here, Saturn fulfills the role of learning through pain. Because Aquarius is an air sign, it is on the mental plane that the native is particularly vulnerable.

The fear and suffering so often associated with Saturn before we come to understand that there is no need to be afraid, are expressed here on the mental and communicative level. Hence these individuals are very sensitive to all sorts of thought structures and ideas (emanating either from the self or from others) on the one hand, and to anything to do with communication and social processes on the other. Especially on account of the latter, people with Saturn in Aquarius have an unconscious need to conceal uncertainty in communicating—either by seclusion from society, or by plunging with a great deal of fuss and bother into various social activities in which they do not really feel at ease but into which they enter to convince self and others how community minded and what good communicators they are.

In all this, the unconscious water element can cause a great deal of trouble. That is to say, unconscious factors periodically surfacing via the fixed cross increase a sense of uncertainty, because Saturn in Aquarius gives little understanding of the attendant emotions. Hence both extreme forms of behavior can be strengthened. However, the nub of the matter is the problem created by the great sensitivity on the communicative plane, so that the person with Saturn in Aquarius can feel very lonely and defensive.

From another point of view, these problems are useful in helping these natives discover the cause of anxieties in this area. They may well succeed in locating deeper frustrations within. If they are able to confront this hidden part, they will be rewarded with a better understanding of self and others. Eventually they will come to see that it makes little difference internally whether they are active participators or remain aloof. They will understand that non-recognition of authority and the simultaneous desire to make one's presence felt are incompatible factors mainly flowing from personal, social and contactual problems, and building an identity can be used as a "launching pad" into the outer world.

URANUS, NEPTUNE AND PLUTO IN AQUARIUS

The tendency to break the mold in the interests of originality (Uranus), the need to refine and dissociate forms and to make them universal (Neptune), and the need for power, confrontation and the transcendence of form (Pluto), are active in Aquarius mainly at the level of mind and communication. Hence great upheavals in thought and communication may be expected to issue from the changing insights within (fixed cross) which, owing to the preponderant nonconformity of a sign (Aquarius) that listens only to its own inner voice, can be either reforming or annihilating in character.

However, these planetary positions will not occur until the end of the twentieth and the beginning of the twenty-first centuries, when we may expect great innovations in society, not so much in terms of its structure (Capricorn) as in general attitudes and in the general type of communal activities and interactions in accordance with the nature of Aquarius. The fixed cross influence also ensures that considerable subjectivity lies concealed behind the very objective seeming stance of this air sign. The influence brings the unconscious element (water) to bear. Therefore, the advent of these planets in Aquarius could herald stirring times.

Chapter Six

Planets in the Element Water

1. Cardinal Water: Cancer

SUN IN CANCER

When the Sun is in a water sign, the way of emotions is the way most in keeping with the native's inmost self. These people develop best through having an emotional relationship with their surroundings and by evaluating everyone and everything in terms of feelings. In Cancer, the element water is combined with the cardinal cross. The psychic energy is directed to the outside, and the assimilation of impressions and handling problems initially talkes place by turning to the outside world and feeling what is going on there. Also, these natives' own roles in the world are important, even though this is not so apparent with members of a water sign. The combination of the water element and the cardinal cross makes these people with Sun in Cancer crave for a significant part to play in the world, and they will certainly be active in it in their own way—for example, as a manipulator who pulls the strings behind the scenes. There is the motherly Cancer woman who cares for her neighborhood and surrounds her family with her protective warmth. There is also the strong-willed woman who has her husband under her emotional or physical control, making him get on in the world for her sake. As time goes by she may become increasingly difficult to please, however, and may frequently resort to domestic bullying to make him achieve more for her.

If the energy of the cardinal cross is blocked or restricted, overcompensation is the likely result. In the worst case we see the emotional person who goes through life tyrannizing and exploiting weaker natures (like the dominating wife already mentioned). However, if the energy flows freely, there are few problems, and Sun in Cancer guarantees warmth, care and protection.

The combination of the sensitivity of a water sign with the extraversion of the cardinal cross makes it hard for Cancer natives to be sure of their inner identity. Possibly they will identify with what is expected of someone in their position by society, although this may not be in keeping with their character. So self-confidence is not always great; generally speaking they gain in assurance when they know they are valued members of the community.

As we have seen, then, there is considerable involvement with the outside world. This involvement makes it difficult for these natives to go against general trends, for that would entail the risk of being cut off from their "base." Add to this the identity problem from which they suffer, and it is not surprising to see Sun in Cancer people attracted to things which are not really in their line. Clearly a certain meddlesomeness can arise out of this, and not always on account of a lack of discretion or improper motives (unless of course the psychic stream is being obstructed somewhere along the way).

Because, as a water sign, Cancer has a direction or orientation towards the inner world (which we must not confuse with the way a fixed sign copes with the world or assimilates his problems!), these natives absorb impressions gained in the outside world and can sympathize with others and give help where possible. Care and sympathy are great virtues, and appreciation of what they bestow in this respect gives Cancers the strength to go on.

Cancer (as a cardinal sign) shows the emotions more readily than do other water signs, due both to the extraversion of the cardinal cross and to the fact that emotions may well disturb the native. Since Cancerians have difficulty in discovering their true identity, feelings can make them vulnerable. By arousing them, others have easy access to their emotional life. This is why Cancerians keep sidestepping—in a vain effort to hide their sensitivity from those around them.

The "crab" is seldom comfortable in a wider and more impersonal social setting. The forcefulness of the cardinal cross in their sign means that, instead of having personal emotions at the mercy of others, the crab wants to create a small, closed environment in which a few people can live under its intimate emotional control and give love and devotion. This place is the home. Here Cancer's dominating influence is usually clearly felt, and because husband, wife, and children instinctively turn to the Cancerian for care and protection, Cancerians have few problems in persuading others that they "always knows what is best" or in making others feel guilty if they ever try to step out of line.

Thus, members of the sign of Cancer are often charged with being overpossessive of spouses, children and the past. Obviously, kith and kin will be important where there is a combination of the water element with the cardinal cross. But, as already indicated, the nature of the water element brings identity problems, it being desirable if not absolutely necessary for those whose birth sign is a water sign to find some fixed point of departure from which they can develop. They clutch at the known, and so we can say that the more insecure they feel, the more significance they will attach to the past. However, if people with Sun in Cancer gradually find their own identity, the past need not play such an important part in life. The natives whose sign is imbued with the influence of the cardinal cross can find it in them to care about the past or the present but not about the uncertain future.

MOON IN CANCER

If need be, the Moon in this placement is more sensitive than the Sun. Direct reactions to external impulses, without the intervention of consciousness, occur at an emotional level when Moon is in Cancer, so that there is a great involvement with the environment (cardinal cross). Because Moon in Cancer influences people's unconscious emotional behavior and the way in which they try to obtain security in uncertain situations, sensitivity is considerable. As soon as something testing or unfamiliar happens, they instinctively withdraw into their (crab's) shell (however, natives of all water signs can shrink into themselves), yet because of the activity of the cardinal cross they continue to occupy themselves with the problem. It is important to do so because on the inside they are concerned with everything that is going on on the outside. Also, they are inclined to respond very emotionally to situations, although they will probably soon regain composure. However, emotions like fear and terror can engage the mind for a long time.

In such a sensitive sign as Cancer, the Moon, which represents our emotional reactions, provides a solid emotional basis, but, as with anything to do with the feelings, the inner life is subject to change. Empathy is great and there are very decided reactions to emotional situations.

Since the emotional life is strongly developed, situations may easily arise in which, at the least affront, these people either enter vigorous protest or else draw back deeply offended. Also, they have no immediate sense of identity. A self-concept is built up only gradually, and the outer world has a big part to play in the process (cardinal cross). Therefore these natives do not tolerate much criticism from the outside world, for to feel at ease they need to find a cosy niche in it somewhere.

Emotional reactions to the outside world often involve an understanding of human needs. All water signs bestow the capacity to care and cherish, but these characteristics are particularly marked with Moon in Cancer, since it is so vitally important for people belonging to this cardinal sign to be actively involved in the environment.

Thinking is awkward for the sign of Cancer and certainly for the Moon, and there can be a deep respect for the apparently effortless manner in which others express themselves so clearly and logically; such fluent expression is not within this native's power. Thinking tends to get into a rut and dwells unduly on pet subjects. Certain patterns of thought which offer emotional security may be very important, helping perhaps to achieve a sense of identity. Although the content of a religion may not always do much for the Moon in Cancer, the bare fact that religion unites people and brings them together, added to the emotional value of a given faith, means that devout, God-fearing people are found among those whose charts have planets in Cancer (but especially when the Sun or Moon is posited in this sign).

The need to play an emotional role and to keep people together on an emotional level is likely to arouse paternal and maternal urges as the case may be. Because the cardinal cross lays so much emphasis on the external world, the person with Moon in Cancer can have feelings that are too much involved in the world. The individual may suppose, in fact, that personal feelings originate inside, whereas they may actually be governed by the standards and values of others. To take a somewhat extreme example: A woman can save her marriage by "standing by" a man whose character is ill matched with her own, who nevertheless suits her because of his social class, income, position in the community and capacity as the father of her children. Social norms can give her feelings which do not arise from within although they do help her function in a way she finds satisfactory. The chance to take an active part in a smoothly working environment is essential to the Cancer Moon sign native's happiness in life.

MERCURY IN CANCER

The urge to arrange and analyze one's feelings has here a purely emotional and subjective background, so that the thought processes are no longer entirely logical and cerebral but are governed by all kinds of emotional influences and internal imagery. Lucid expression is not the sole consideration. The person with Mercury in Cancer is often good at picturesque description and unconsciously endeavors to evoke a particular emotional reaction in others when talking or writing on certain subjects.

As already mentioned, analysis is guided by feelings, which is not to say that the conclusions reached are unimportant. However, the person with Mercury in Cancer is liable to forget that, because the sign is oriented toward the outer world, he is inclined to think the conclusions reached are valid for everyone and that all people are alike in the way their minds work.

The way he puts two and two together has an emotional basis as well. He can make connections between facts and phenomena without extensive and logical analysis. His conclusions are already contained in his feelings, but this causes him problems when asked to give a step-by-step account of how those conclusions were reached. Also, because rigorous logical and mathematical thinking are not his strongest point (he may even decry them!), he may seem to be a slow thinker. It is not every subject that will take his fancy: to be able to tackle it, he must find something in it or in the way it is approached which stirs his emotions. If his emotions are stirred, his memory is retentive; if not, he soon forgets. Emotional things and events which touch the feelings, whether they have to do with today or yesterday, mean a lot to him, and he likes to contemplate and relive them.

That the individual with Mercury in Cancer is sometimes reproached with being too conservative is quite understandable, since the thinking inspired by a water sign is involved in the building of an identity, a matter which people belonging to water signs usually find more difficult than do folks belonging to certain other signs. This, in combination with the fact that feelings are directed toward the outer world, may mean that whatever is tried and trusted and makes them feel safe is important to maintain as far as they are concerned. Thinking which is strongly emotional and subjective is therefore quite liable to be conservative.

Since the mind is so imaginative and is so adept at thinking in pictures and symbolic representations, the native readily picks up the emotional content of fairy tales, myths and legends, Arthurian romances and other folklore. In short, this native takes pleasure in all sorts of narrations and reports which seem to have "something in them" even though the material sometimes defies the laws of logic.

The cardinal cross, with its involvement in the external world, poses people with Mercury in Cancer some problems when it comes to making decisions or passing judgment. It is vitally important for them to have the emotional life continually fed by impulses coming from the outside world. They do not like to have this flow disrupted, and so find it hard to express opinions that are not acceptable in their particular circle; nor is it easy for them to criticize error, even though inside they may be very irritated by it.

Where the mental energy is blocked or inhibited, these natives may feel even more dependent on the environment and may find it hard to think for themselves. On the other hand they may, from time to time, attempt to take the lead among their companions and to interest others in things in which they are emotionally involved. They may even try to ram opinions down your throat. However, they may equally retire into a personal fantasy world rather than coming to terms with themselves on the communicative plane (water).

VENUS IN CANCER

The human need, represented by Venus, for beauty, comfort and security both on the plane of matter and on that of emotions, is more frankly emotional when the planet is in Cancer. The values seen in life will be emotional ones, which these natives will readily adopt for peace of mind. Therefore, the environment and the external world in general will have an important part to play (cardinal cross), but not overwhelmingly so. What does on in the external world is significant to these natives but, because they belong to a water sign, they will not immediately plunge into its various activities. Nevertheless, the effect of Venus in Cancer is quite unmistakable. When the influence of Venus is exerted in a water sign, these natives usually need to feel close to other people. In Cancer, the action of the cardinal cross enhances this feeling, and the results can be very constructive because the native has plenty of empathy with others and is ready to lend them emotional support. If there is no proper outlet for this impulse, however, the energy of the cardinal cross will eventually enable it to break through, and the native may wrap himself or herself around others in a stifling way emotionally.

Harmony and beauty are usually sought in a restricted circle of acquaintances or in surroundings where the retiring sensitivity of water can be at ease. The need for a warm union and for harmony in an intimate atmosphere can, if obstructed, lead to great self-consciousness and the desire to remain in the protection of the home or perhaps to cling to the shreds of a union that is no longer what it was out of a fear of being left alone.

The emotions of Venus in Cancer are very much regulated by the environment, from which—owing to the influence of the cardinal cross—these emotional impulses come. These impulses may almost unconsciously determine their standards, making them likely to be conventional about behavior. Therefore, these natives are not easily led within a relationship to do things which would not meet with general approval since this could isolate them from their main source of emotional comfort. Nevertheless, it is also true to say that Venus in Cancer people can learn to be less dependent on the outside world (when, for example, the horoscope as a whole gives a greater awareness of personal identity), and are able to express the warmth and care within them without needing a feedback of impulses from outside. Then behavior may sometimes become more Bohemian.

People belonging to a water sign seldom make the first move, so that, with Venus in Cancer, we must not expect a great deal of initiative in spite of the fact that Cancer is a cardinal sign. However, these people do make their feelings known—the cardinal sign does not belie its nature.

MARS IN CANCER

Mars, as the innate drive to distiguish oneself from others, will operate in an emotional way in Cancer. The activities of life are primarily determined by all kinds of emotional impulses which may not always be reliable or well considered. Sometimes there is scarcely any perceptible activity, since for Mars in Cancer even mental image building, dreaming and fantasizing can represent genuine activity.

By manipulating other people's emotions, those with Mars in Cancer are enabled to feel superior (the cardinal cross always give the desire to be someone in the community!). On the other hand, certain things which have great emotional value for them can rouse them from comparative passivity and turn them into fierce fighters. In general, however, they prefer to avoid conflict so as not to upset their emotional relationship with the outside world.

When the environment is disturbed, these people are disturbed. But since they are much in favor of keeping to the tried and trusted as they are anxious to establish themselves as distinct individuals, their influence can restore harmony as well as destroy it.

Here is another planetary placement which indicates a strong duality: the retiring nature of the water element and its capacity for absorbing things into itself versus orientation toward the surroundings and a desire to play some part out there. Although Mars in Cancer may not energize the natives to be terribly active (except when moved by some emotional compulsion), they can certainly motivate others to get on with the job. An example here is that of a wife who is the driving force behind her husband, who monitors his work, spare-time activities, achievements, progress and so on, because of a strong emotional attachment to him; who also, if he tries to frustrate her, can tyrannize him because her driving energy is bound to find expression. On the other hand, there is the possibility that thwarting the individual will create a total blockage so that all external activity is abandoned.

When shedding its influence from Cancer, Mars, as the aggressive form of the instinct of self-preservation, can act purely through the feelings. On the other hand, the self-assertiveness imparted by the planet may lead the native to step on other people's toes. There is a certain measure of emotional security required for Mars to be able to function. Reactions from the outside may arouse too many emotions and may even paralyze the energy—it is all too much for Mars in Cancer. The individual may then look inward and become occupied with daydreaming and fantasizing. When the cardinal cross influence turns once more to face the external world, it is likely that this Mars will have set sights too high and will be doomed to disappointment, or that everyday life will seem no more than a pale reflection of what it might have been, so that it no longer provides the necessary incentive to do anything useful.

We see then that individuals who have Mars in Cancer like to stand out from their surroundings and yet involve themselves from an emotional point of view. They will be very sensitive to this duality in everyday life.

JUPITER IN CANCER

Here the need for spiritual and religious values has an emotional background. The meaning contained in these values is not as important, at least in the beginning, as the sense of security they afford. They hold a community together and can create that sense of unity that is so important to anyone influenced by the sign of Cancer. As members of the cardinal cross, these natives are primarily inclined to share feelings with their immediate circle—in this instance religious and spiritual feelings. Whether or not these feelings are very elevated hardly seems to matter; even if they become an adherent of some noble faith, its main attraction will be the group solidarity it gives.

Jovian expansiveness is governed by the emotions when the planet is in Cancer, but is also directed toward the outside world (cardinal cross). Therefore, the natives can make good use of the ability to feel for others or to come to their assistance in various ways. They may heal, help to solve problems, encourage others to improve their social position and so on. Gratitude makes it all worth while for this Jupiter. Responses from the environment are, so to speak, fuel for the crab. Should Jupiter in Cancer be impeded (by other factors in the horoscope) from expressing its influence freely, it will nevertheless be impelled into some form of manifestation by the influence of the cardinal cross. Then there can be a certain meddlesomeness under the guise of trying to be helpful, or a fanatical espousal of some religious cause: that represented by the established church, say, or by some sect or so on. Individuals with Jupiter in Cancer generally seek to enter emotionally into the world around them in order to be able to play, preferably, a helping and an improving part in it.

SATURN IN CANCER

When Saturn is in Cancer, emotions are something of a weak chink in the individual's armor. The process of learning through pain takes place in the emotional life. The native learns (in a frequently painful manner) to know personal limitations, and will integrate the difficult experiences in life into the developing ego. This person has a great need for emotional security and seeks it in the world outside (due to the cardinal cross influence). But because the search for emotional security is so compulsive and is associated with all kinds of anxieties (such as the anxiety that security will never be found), the behavior toward the external world is dualistic. On one hand there is a strong desire for emotional participation, but on the other the defense mechanism makes it hard or even impossible to be a participant. Anxiety, and feelings of loneliness or emotional inadequacy, make the native inclined to erect a wall around the feelings so securely that anything which might injure them is kept out. The world, of course, reacts unfavorably to being kept at arm's length, and this increases the native's sense of isolation. And even should it react more favorably and more in keeping with personal values, this native might fail to realize it. What is more, a personal need to share warmth with other people is obstructed by this selfsame wall. The outer world then sees this person as cold, unfeeling, remote, etc., but in actuality nothing could be less true. There really is a very strong need to give and receive warmth and to experience the attachment of an emotional alliance—but there are obstacles to be overcome.

Now, if the native gains the insight that personal anxiety arises from an inner uncertainty which has no roots in anything going on outside, Saturn in Cancer will then be in a position to break down the wall to reveal a true-hearted, uncomplicated, warm-blooded person who is neither repelled nor overcome by emotions. But, as long as this happy state of affairs is not in existence, the individual can either remain fenced off from the environment or keep clutching at it more and more desperately, so that others feel an indefinable "heaviness" in his or her presence, a heaviness that will also burden the soul until the restricting influences are removed.

URANUS, NEPTUNE AND PLUTO IN CANCER

All three planets have transited Cancer this century, placing the unconscious activities of the emotional life of our species under various types of pressure. In fact they have brought about certain changes in these activities. Uranus as the urge to break the mold of form and to be original, Neptune as the need to blur the edges of form, to refine and to dissociate it, and Pluto as the need for power, confrontation and the transcendence of form, operated purely emotionally in Cancer, but also in relation to the environment. The first to transit Cancer this century was the planet Neptune, which, in its early years, gave society greater refinement but also a decadent sensitivity and lack of realism. Special emphasis was laid on stylishness, as in the art nouveau. Pluto rolled over everything to do with feelings of comfort and safety; and so it is not surprising that many whose feelings were crushed by two world wars had Pluto in Cancer. However, Pluto in this sign can also draw on hidden reserves of strength, and people were able to show what they were made of in difficult times. During this period, humanity was confronted with radical changes in the emotional impulses which tend to shape society. (The ingress of Pluto into Leo produced a generation which must learn to shape itself in a new way, with new, almost untried values. The individual will become important again, as soon as the activities initiated by Pluto in Cancer have completely broken up the old ground.)

Finally, Uranus built on the foundation laid down by Pluto in Cancer. The need to be original can, when charged with the emotions, produce all kinds of uncertainty but, by the same token, can stimulate the search for new forms of emotional security. Changed attitudes can lead to rethinking of the structure of the family and of its social significance: the individual has been given more freedom to develop separately within the emotional unit. The danger is that the family is no longer able to offer the warmth it formerly offered and that its bonds will become too slack. This generation will take a fresh look at a situation in which there is much to gain and, regrettably, much to lose.

2. FIXED WATER: SCORPIO

SUN IN SCORPIO

The nature of people with the Sun in Scorpio is both deep (fixed cross) and emotional (water). The fixed cross influence directs the flow of psychic energy inward to the unconscious, and all the contents of the unconscious are periodically brought to the surface, chewed over and assimilated. The function of feeling, represented by water, plays the main part in this assimilation process. Sun sign Scorpio natives approach the world through feelings, judging situations, events and (last but not least) people by means of their feelings. The water element makes Scorpio very sensitive to impulses coming from the outside world. In the beginning anyway, the ego feels rather exposed, as if things were "coming at it" from all sides—whether this is really so or not. Yet, such is the power of the fixed cross influence that these natives are able to absorb these influences which so strongly affect them; in this way they try to come to terms with influences emotionally. Because air is the inferior element that is brought into the open by the fixed cross, Scorpios often give the impression of being deep thinkers (air represents the function of thinking), which is not entirely untrue. However, their feelings are the basis of their thinking, which is never so strongly differentiated as their feelings are. Consequently, these natives, like members of any of the fixed signs, take their experiences deep into themselves and require time to assimilate. Being in a water sign that, as a feminine sign, does not readily let them come out with the things which occupy their minds, they can make a "brooding" impression. One can sense that they are thinking about something they want to "get off their chest."

Owing to the uncommunicativeness of the fixed cross, it is very hard for Scorpio natives to express feelings, which is why people belonging to this sign are sometimes thought to be mentally retarded when they are not. The coldness, the apparent alienation, are really masks for a deep almost unimaginably differentiated emotional life. The feelings of those with Sun in Scorpio are very exposed in the main, and therefore they can sometimes be very fierce and easily aroused for what seems to be no good reason. They manifest aggression and the sudden violent reactions are really expressions of hidden insecurity. The element water, which is so easily impressed and influenced by the outside world, in combination with the fixed cross, which is continually allowing unconscious factors to slip into the conscious mind, can make these natives feel insecure and can cause them to cling to a real or assumed identity. Hence it is understandable that people with Sun in Scorpio are often ambitious and competitive and are likely to have a sense of their own importance. They are continually in search of their own worth and their own identity in some way or other. By this we mean that their self-assertiveness is not rigidly channeled into obtaining an important position in society (although this is very possible, of course) but is spread to cover such areas as those of leisure pursuits, the family, everyday life and even the world of the occult.

The inferior function, thinking, which, through the influence of the fixed cross, acts compulsively every now and again, often gives Scorpio natives the need to set things in order and to analyze them. However, their inner path, the path that suits the development of their personalities best, lies through the field of emotions. Periods of thought can add depth to feelings but, if continued too long, can have an undermining effect and throw up very unsettled emotions. Therefore Scorpio natives, all too aware of personal insecurity, are ready to go looking for insecurity in others in the hope of unmasking it. In this endeavor they will often succeed, but run the risk of suspecting that people are worse than they really are. Feelings, which in many instances flow without interference, are in this case mixed with the inferior function of thinking to the extent that these natives become very subjective; and their analyses or conclusions are not always logical because their conscious minds have so little grip on their own thought processes (which are largely in the hands of emotions).

People with Sun in Scorpio can be very persistent in efforts to get to know and understand self and others. Perseverance in these efforts leads to a "spiral downward" until they are satisfied that they have arrived where they want to be. In the process, they can sometimes display an "all or nothing" attitude, which, when thwarted, can turn to violence, destructiveness, lust for power and so on. However, if the energy is diverted into positive channels, the result can be a deep insight into people and life.

The double uncertainty (harassment from the unconscious and sensitivity toward the outside world) puts Scorpio natives quickly on guard; they may seem to be suspicious, and sometimes are. Another related form of behavior is that Scorpios will withdraw into a shell when faced with an experience that is difficult to digest, or when made the butt of an unkind remark, and the like. These are things they must first assimilate. For a long while they may appear to be unmoved, but in fact inside they are seething with rage and turning everything over mentally at top speed. It is owing to this intense inner activity that they are blamed for being egotistical and thinking only of self. Anyone who understands the critical way in which Scorpio approaches, experiences and assimilates things knows better. The native is not consciously egotistical; it is even necessary to spend time alone as much as possible so as to avoid being thrown off the scent. Nevertheless, once committed to a certain idea or decision, Scorpio is not afraid to let it be known what is stood for. In defending emotional values Scorpio can be as obstinate as a Taurus. Obviously, there will be strong sympathies and antipathies. What we have said really amounts to this—Scorpio natives draw deep from the experiences the world has to offer, yet with feelings of misgiving which they try to overcome, whatever the cost.

MOON IN SCORPIO

The unconscious, emotional behavior of individuals with Moon in Scorpio is intensely active. When the Moon is in a water sign, the emotional nature is already strongly developed, but in Scorpio there is the added intensity of the fixed cross, which can give great richness and depth to the life of the feelings. Yet these natives scarcely ever expose their emotional life to the light of day. The sense of uncertainty so often linked with this position of the Moon will usually prevent them from doing so. The fixed cross keeps on confronting emotions with the inferior function of thinking. This can evoke feelings of insufficiency, which are so pernicious to the Moon in its diligent search for security. And so a great deal of uncertainty attends the very creation of certainty. Perhaps this is why traditional astrology was not particularly impressed by this placement and tended to overlook the constructive (though still not easy) sides of these natives' character.

Individuals with Moon in Scorpio will try to exact more than a pound of flesh in any matter in which they have an emotional stake. They are ready to go through fire for it. Because of their uncertainty, however, they like to be highly regarded and value loyalty. Since they are mainly interested in inner security, they don't go looking merely for a reward. It is the *feeling* of being important that matters (unlike the member of the cardinal cross, who is anxious to see what sort of a figure he cuts in society!).

If the energy of Moon in Scorpio is obstructed in this regard, or if they are misunderstood by other people, this can very easily touch on a raw spot, leading these natives to retire into themselves while nursing injured feelings. A great sensitivity on the one hand, and uncertainty on the other, make them suspicious and wary, like the Sun sign Scorpio. The fixed cross can aggravate emotionally difficult experiences and protract the assimilation process, since emotional insecurity in combination with an intensified inner life has to be satisfied: now, the insecurity cannot be emphasized with impunity, and it must be pointed out that people with Moon in Scorpio really have problems. This is why, even after a long time, natives can hit out hard to avenge a real or fancied injury when the other party may well have forgotten what it is all about. Gratitude for acts of kindness is equally long lived. They can therefore prove to be very devoted and true, but must overcome feelings of uncertainty and other impediments before they can say what is is their hearts.

The need to be "a somebody" is great, and if this need is thwarted it will probably make itself felt in one way or another. Problems may arise through overcompensations which are uncomfortable for others. These may be directed against the community at large or may expend their full force in the more intimate atmosphere or the home. In the latter, some individuals dominate over spouses and offspring and if children are wayward or disrespectful, Moon in Scorpio offers corporal punishment. Thus you see the angry man who batters his wife and thrashes his children, or the bullying woman who likes to give her weak husband or children a good smacking to show that she is boss. In extreme cases, we have the so-called "crime of passion," which may sometimes be a desperate attempt to repair a badly dented ego image—an ego image which was especially valued because it had been formed with so much difficulty. Sudden bursts of aggression may backfire, so that the native feels more insecure than ever, and the whole problem is often compounded because those around fail to sense the way in which the Scorpio Moon is inwardly seething long before the outburst.

Individuals with Moon in Scorpio need to put a lot of feeling into life but, in doing so, often undermine their own position. Therefore, they require too much understanding and appreciation for whatever they are doing. This is the engine that keeps them working. They need to be in emotional communication with people who value knowing them.

MERCURY IN SCORPIO

The urge to classify and analyze experiences, such as is represented by Mercury, has an emotional background when the planet is in Scorpio. The arranging and analyzing processes are pushed by the action of the fixed cross into the depths of the psyche where they are confronted by the inferior element—in this case air. There is little differentiation about the thinking function when in this position, but everything tends to be sorted out on an emotional basis even though logic is used. This means that these individuals can go to extremes. Those with this placement are able, on the basis of feelings, to give very detailed accounts (subjective perhaps but nevertheless well worked out) of person, event or situation; the placement can also be responsible for such things as slavery to facts, hobbyhorses and the use of the gathered and analyzed facts to achieve personal power.

Owing to the action of the fixed cross, to the sense of uncertainty and to the need to get to know things, analysis is taken further and further until the subject in hand has been exhausted. This is done, not as Virgo natives would do it—by chopping everything up into small pieces in order to chew them over—but by so to say "brewing" the whole and by reflecting on it, by reliving it emotionally until illumination suddenly comes. This insight is then so deeply anchored that they are no longer able to give it up. These people may appear to be completely passive and inert during the process but are really very active internally.

The same mechanism insures that people with Mercury in Scorpio will defend at all costs any opinion adopted, and of course the more emotion invested in this opinion the fiercer they will be. When they feel a certain degree of doubt in the matter (for example when confronted by the inferior element), they may even propagate an opinion vigorously to convince themselves of its truth rather than abandon it as untenable!

If they can bring themselves to guide the mental processes with a steady hand, however, they can gain some profound insights, at the cost perhaps of acquiring a certain cynicism which they are not afraid to betray by word or gesture. Folks may have to get used to their uncanny ability to lay a finger right on the sore spot.

As an inward-looking, emotionally activated investigator, individuals with Mercury in Scorpio are well suited to research that digs below the surface in parapsychology and the occult, looking for hidden keys of knowledge, etc. They may follow the lead set by the inferior function of thinking, but they will probably notice that when they go by sudden hunches or brainwaves, they will get further than many others do. Feelings are their main assets, and thinking is best done in retrospect.

In the way that they arrange facts and events in thinking and speaking, you will see they are really on a search for self. This can make them seem more or less polarized. However, through this polarization they see themselves in contrast to others, and by means of verbal contests (whether or not barbed with psychological venom) they can try to prove their own abilities, identities or even superiorities. Given these characteristics, they can stir up a heap of trouble in local or central government, but may also serve as spokesmen for minority interests which are in danger of being suppressed or ignored. What people with Mercury in Scorpio have to say always springs ultimately from the emotions.

VENUS IN SCORPIO

The human need for material and emotional satisfaction is very intense in Scorpio. The natives' emotional lives are strong but unsettled; so the Venusian need for safety comes under considerable pressure when the planet is in this position. A need for safety implies a sense of its lack, and the uncertainty of Scorpio can overcompensate in such a way that undue emphasis on emotional security can endanger that very security. In practice this can result in the jealous possessiveness of a partner so often ascribed to Venus in Scorpio. This intense jealousy arises from the sense of insecurity. Wherever there is insecurity there we have fertile soil for jealous feelings. On the other hand, where there is a sense of security, there is no need for jealousy. For fear a mate may be lost to some rival, Venus in Scorpio will sometimes persuade the mate to be unsociable for Venus' sake. Venus here loves and hates with equal passion, yet is often touchingly faithful—faithful unto death as the saying goes.

Venus, as the symbolic hand outstretched to receive a warm and positive response from others, has problems in Scorpio. People with Venus here need to protect themselves from life's emotional weather, and draw aloofness around them like a waterproof cape and their half-extended hands are concealed in its folds, so to speak. The cape of aloofness looks cold and impervious enough to deter a close encounter, but inside it there is plenty of warmth—and room enough for two.

The need for harmony and beauty is experienced internally in the main, and hardly a hint of it escapes to the outside. Opposites are reconciled and united inside these individuals for the most part. The fixed cross imparts a sense of uncertainty into this water sign, and can quickly upset the normal balance. For example, it may make it difficult for a man or woman to accept that unity in marriage in which they lose themselves in one another and are absorbed by the greater whole. The native's insecurity creates a longing for, and yet a dread of, being stripped of selfishness and of entering the service of love. He or she may well resist this and opt for separation or divorce or look for subtle (or forcible) ways to manipulate the union. Again, where there is rather less fear of marital obligations yet still an unwillingness to make a total commitment, the instinctive longing to surrender is confined to the erotic level so that the individual becomes sexually demanding.

The tension brought about by the craving for emotional warmth and by the hesitation over crossing the inner threshold can be released in artistic pursuits, if we understand "artistic" in the widest sense of the word. Being creative can alleviate the pangs of emotional distress.

MARS IN SCORPIO

In the individual who has Mars in Scorpio, the innate drive to stand apart and to distinguish oneself from others, and the desire to develop and emphasize one's own individuality, operate in an inward-looking (fixed cross) and emotional (water) way. The high degree of emotionality gives the person with Mars in this sign the ability to put full weight behind any project in which feelings are involved. But the fixed cross influence induces this person to suck things inward so to speak. Mars here can even become so obsessed by a certain subject as to be unable to think of anything else for a time. Obviously, the energy concentrated on this one point is likely to be very powerful. Therefore, Mars is a force to be reckoned with in society for good or ill. In fact, Mars in Scorpio indicates the sort of person who would face destruction rather than yield an inch when fighting for a cherished cause.

The executive energy of Mars has great intensity where this placement is concerned, because whatever the fixed cross "seizes" it is loathe to release. These natives will do anything for those to whom they are emotionally attached (water element), but can fly at anybody for whom they feel an antipathy.

Just as with other planets in Scorpio, Mars too suffers from the general uncertainty and the need to keep searching for something. The fixed cross influence imparts an undermining effect to the inferior function, whereas Mars likes to be sure of his ground. Hence Mars in Scorpio is liable to overcompensate. Perhaps this is the reason why traditional astrology assigned to this placement of Mars considerable self-importance, aggression and ambition and a need for the native to prove his or her sexual prowess. The latter characteristic, although frequently expressed, forms part of a wider need for self-assertion in the face of inner uncertainty and is therefore no isolated phenomenon. The native does not always turn his or her partner into a sexual slave, although the possiblitiy is always there. On the contrary, the tendency to reserve implicit in the water sign-fixed cross combination can give great self-control; in which case, the influence of Mars in Scorpio is not noticeably bad. However, the individual may well be seething under a calm exterior, and when the pressure builds up beyond a certain point, there will be a devastating explosion and old grievances which have been stored away will come hurling into the open.

When Mars is in Scorpio, the energy imparted by the planet and the desire to be someone of importance are prone to be diverted by overemotionality and the uncertainty of the fixed cross. Consequently, self-assertion is liable to be greater than when Mars is in other signs. If these natives are thwarted, overcompensation can be quite severe. If, on the other hand, they are able to put good qualities to constructive use, we see people who display concentration, resolution, reliability and self-control, all of which can be used in everyday social life to overcome initial uncertainties.

JUPITER IN SCORPIO

Although not all astrological textbooks speak well of the placement of Jupiter in this sign, experience teaches that it can bring long-term benefits to the inner life. In this position, the normal expansive influence of Jupiter in material things is often deferred; perhaps this is why the placement is not too highly regarded. In a need for enlargement, the native absorbs personal experiences deep down. He works not in length but in depth and, during the span of a human life, can acquire great inner wisdom. The fact that Scorpio is one of the water signs suggests that the native will be interested in psychological matters and will want to gain an insight into the motivations of self and others and, finally, into the meaning of life itself. Spiritual and religious values are formed along these lines. He can see through outward show because, as far as he is concerned, everything turns on an inner hub. Nevertheless, when the psychic energy is obstructed, it may well happen that the native attempts to transmit inner values in some kind of display, because of an uncertainty of the question or the "message" and wants to "wrap it up" a bit.

Confrontation with the inferior element keeps the native seeking. Once emotionally convinced of something, it can be rationalized and the native can keep digging for fresh facts to support it. The resulting insights can give an idea of how to manipulate people (in a subtle way); for the person with Jupiter in Scorpio, while seeking to understand everything, seeks above all to find his own role in life. Under the influence of the fixed cross he will keep chewing things over in his mind. He may miss one or two external factors by so doing, but he will never miss the kernel of the matter. His interest in the hidden helps to insure this.

If this investigative energy is blocked or frustrated, the person with Jupiter in Scorpio may overcompensate too freely. The principle of expansion will begin to show itself, and because the native's own situation is uncertain, he can start peering with unashamed impudence into someone else's soul and can put their life on the dissecting table despite all protests. And, since Scorpio is an emotional water sign, he can be very subjective about what he is doing, so that he sees his own faults and failings in his victims and loads them with moralizing advice, thus adding insult to injury.

Whatever the case, the expansive energy and the craving for religious and spiritual values have a deeply emotional background, and it is with deep feeling that the native goes in diligent search of self and of the meaning of existence. As the search proceeds, Jupiter in Scorpio can develop profound insights.

SATURN IN SCORPIO

Representing the process of learning through pain, Saturn displays its limiting action here too, especially in matters affecting the emotions. On the one hand, the feelings are necessary for gradually building up consciousness, and yet on the other hand, they are precisely the weak point in the individual's makeup. Saturn in a water sign represents great sensitiveness on the emotional plane. The fixed cross influence sucks every experience inward and retains it for a long time. This sensitiveness makes Saturn in this sign (as in all water signs) inclined to build a wall around the feelings for protection against emotional uncertainty and against the effects of difficult experiences. Saturn succeeds, we might say, in locking out problems—they hardly seem to have any effect. At the same time, however, Saturn shuts out all the warmth and affection offered by others, and keeps all feelings and personal warmth imprisoned in a bastion. The danger for people with Saturn in Scorpio is, therefore, that the defense mechanism will override any attempt to make genuine human contacts. This means that loneliness can set in if these individuals are unable to break through the "safety-first spiral." Improverishment of contacts will gnaw at them inside, and because they are fixated on feelings, they will be brought face to face with their obtrusive inferior element, which they will try to control only to find they have given it the opportunity to control them. People with Saturn in Scorpio can often give the impression of being very cerebral and rational if not cold and unfeeling; whereas everything is concentrated on their own inner emotions, and this makes them seem cold.

The uncertainty arising from this spiral can produce many types of overcompensation. There may be a desire to get out of the way of all possible confrontations (for example by entering a monastery for other than religious motives); on the other hand, there may be an uncontrollable urge for these natives to prove themselves. Quite often this position inclines people to be self-assertive; they will work hard to make a solid career.

The sign Scorpio is frequently associated with sexuality. In sexuality individuals both experience their own limitations and become intensely wrapped up in someone else; in other words, they are confronted by the question of how far their own personality extends and of where another's personality begins, interacts with their own and becomes perceptible. Saturn emphasizes this underlying question, which can be raised in so many different ways, of which sexuality is only one. Feelings, the role of the other party, etc. are weak points. Therefore, Saturn in this sign can display a number of divergent overcompensations, from complete celibacy, in which the sex life is renounced, to the role of a Don Juan making a fresh "conquest" every night. Both are forms of escapism: running away from sex and continually trying to prove oneself are expressions of a deep-rooted uncertainty and sensitiveness. Of course many intermediate forms are possible.

To sum up then, individuals with Saturn in Scorpio need their feelings in order to give shape to consciousness but, at the same time, feelings are their main weakness. And the fact that Scorpio is a fixed cross sign makes matters worse. If they can overcome problems to give shape to their emotional life, they may gain profound understanding and a life lived to some purpose due to awareness of the part they can play in society. However, both the planet Saturn and the sign Scorpio tend to encourage overcompensations, so that there are some severe internal battles to be fought before, as is entirely possible, these natives win their personal campaign.

URANUS, NEPTUNE AND PLUTO IN SCORPIO

The need to break form and the urge to be original (Uranus), the need to refine form, to dissolve it and to make it universal (Neptune), and the desire for power, confrontation and the transcendence of form (Pluto), will express themselves very intensely in the sign Scorpio. The fixed cross will dredge up considerable amounts of what lies in the depths of the human psyche via its inferior function and, in doing so, will add more insecurity but also more power and intensity to these transsaturnian planets. Owing to the emotional dimension imparted to them by this water sign, these factors can have a transforming but also a very destructive effect.

To begin with, when Uranus and Neptune enter this sign they release all sorts of mass emotional reactions. Although there is nothing new in this, there is something new in the manner in which the emotions are expressed. There is a growing interest in the hidden, in things not immediately accessible to the "five senses," such as, for instance, occult and parapsychological phenomena.

A negative side of these planets in Scorpio is the increased receptivity for what wells up from within—dreams and illusions. The fixed cross influence can aggravate the problem since it makes the individual disinclined to heed advice from outside. Everything must be personally experienced.

Uranus followed Neptune into this sign to give a growing need for an independent, unrestricted identity and for the free development of the individuality. Civil disobedience has increased. The inner voice calls and the emotions troop after it. Hence, with Pluto in Scorpio there are conflicts between lesser and greater interests: whether it is a case of the majority against the minority or the minority against the majority hardly matters. Whatever is given the highest value by the inner emotions (fixed cross and water sign!) is defended tooth and nail. The era is one of renewal, of change and of the setting of a new course, but also of the release of tensions which have always been kept bottled up. The result can be both good and bad. Children with this placement are continually confronted by the unrest of the period and bear the mark of it. The energies of the planets can increase this unrest because their character of bending or breaking makes them difficult to control, but they can also produce improvements to relieve the sense of dissatisfaction as the native learns to come to terms with tensions and to use them creatively and constructively. And so people with planets in this sign can, by using their own inner resources, make significant contributions both to the demolition and to the reconstruction of society and the world such as they experience them internally.

3. MUTABLE WATER: PISCES

SUN IN PISCES

Initially, people who have the Sun in Pisces have a low level of awareness. The water element emphasizes emotions so that they react strongly to impulses from the environment. The mutable cross is not directly concerned with thorough assimilation (as is found for example in Scorpio) nor with earnest adjustment to the outside world (as in Cancer). The Sun in Pisces is caught, so to speak, between the two. Because these natives are not set in a single direction, they can be many sided, but because they are easily influenced and are inclined to passivity (the water element), they will be (too) ready to follow some path that is not suitable simply because it is the path of someone admired or who is a close acquaintance. Therefore, individuals with Sun in Pisces will take some time to discover their own identity, and what generally happens is that they take another look at what they thought they were but do not seem to be. Consciousness is formed by a kind of delayed process. So it is difficult to advise these natives on how best to be themselves; they will experience having a "foreign" identity before acquiring their own. This is in fact the way in which they develop; it is how they naturally behave. To offset the problems involved in working out who they really are and what they really want, they also have some immediately usable faculties. One of these is the ability imparted by a great sensitivity, by a relatively slow ego development and by a poor sense of identity to get inside someone else's skin and to appreciate unconsciously exactly what that other person needs. Hence Sun in Pisces has an outstanding opportunity to engage successfully in relief and welfare work. Pisces is sympathetic, can come to terms with the other person's point of view and can help in an understanding way. The native, because of the mutable cross influence, does not understand this empathy. Pisces has an unstructured way of assimilating things: Assimilation can occur both in the personal inner world and in the outer world, and the dualism implicit in mutability makes the very unconscious water element still less controlled than usual.

Nevertheless, the mutable cross is well adapted to assist the interchange between the conscious and the unconscious; so that with the Sun in Pisces we often see natives have no great need to distinguish between fantasy and reality. They can live as in a dream and dream as if dreaming were life itself, and with this they are perfectly satisfied. But if they do not come to learn that there is a difference between the two, a difference that they must know in order to hold their own in society, they will run the risk that the personality will not continue to develop and the unconscious mind, with all its contents, will gradually take possession of the conscious mind to produce a great measure of impersonality. And then these natives will easily serve (mutable cross influence) ideas and trends they happen to encounter in life, as ideas accost both their impersonal and "unconscious" consciousness.

In relationships with their fellow men they can use this impersonality when it comes to lending a helping hand for example. Pisces people may turn out to be real Christians (outwardly); people who, without obtruding themselves, help others modestly and devotedly. However, they may possibly be overcome by the things in their unconscious, and the danger then is that they will identify themselves with these things so that, instead of seeing themselves as Christians, they behave as if they were Christ. It goes without saying that there is a whole range of intermediate positions between these two extremes.

The desire for change invariably associated with the mutable cross manifests itself on the emotional plane in Pisces, so there is a great longing for variety in emotional experiences. It should be noted, however, that this longing is certainly not altogether tied in with what is going on in the "real" world, for the world of inner experience has at least as great a pull, and a shortage of external impressions will serve only to strengthen the activities of the soul. All the same, this mutability is the cause of frequent changes of mood.

As in each water sign, the Sun in Pisces makes the native very sensitive to atmospheres and undercurrents of feeling in the immediate surroundings, and he will unconsciously adapt to them. Yet the action of the mutable cross will make him uncertain whether these impressions come from his own unconscious or from that of others; hence, on the one hand, he gets little help in becoming conscious of his own identity, and, on the other hand, he runs the risk of taking upon himself the burdens of the whole community. Whereas someone with the Sun in Cancer participates with and sympathizes with others without losing identity, the Pisces native can easily be absorbed in other people's troubles because it is hard for him to tell what is his and what is not. Therefore, he may suffer from feelings of guilt which have nothing to do with him but are nevertheless very real.

His sensitivity to atmospheres and feelings, combined with his strong susceptibility to the influence of others, make the Pisces subject open to unreal things as well as to real things. He is so wedded to the lady Imagination dwelling in his rich fantasy world that he becomes involved in all sorts of things beyond the borders of our matter-of-fact universe. On the one hand, this can make him superstitious, but, on the other hand, the person with this type of sensitivity can grow into a great mystic, a visionary who out of a deep religious feeling appreciates and intuitively understands the laws of the unseen. Thus the Sun in Pisces can express itself in many different ways, from drifting, dreaming impracticality to a deep and universal insight, in which the native is no longer bound to his own tiny ego but finds his role in the great whole, in the cosmos.

Any obstruction of the psychic energy can have the effect of encouraging overcompensation—in this instance by reinforcing extreme attitudes. In the Pisces native, the unconscious will always play a part, either in a passive and dreamy frame of mind, or in compulsively "impersonal" personal behavior in which he gives the impression of no longer attaching any importance to his own identity and opinion. He may try to convert his fellowmen to a set of values which are at one and the same time subjective *and* collective. Nowadays such collective and subjective values can attach themselves to some exotic religion, to a sect, to an idea and so on, and the native becomes their devotee. Be that as it may, he has a need to form his own identity through emotional experiences, an identity that is established slowly because the mutable cross urges him to pass through all possibilities (since it gives a need for both inner and outer change) before he comes to a conscious realization of the depths within himself.

MOON IN PISCES

In their unconscious emotional behavior people with Moon in Pisces are very sensitive and inward looking (due to the influence of the water element), yet the mutable cross implants a great need for change without, however, leading them to put personal safety at risk.

Because the Moon introduces further emotionality into the psychic mechanism determining our emotional reaction to the environment, Moon in Pisces makes these natives very sensitive, suggestible and often easily influenced. There is a need for safety (Moon), which is mainly sought on the emotional plane (water) and in emotional exchange with the environment. Just as we found with the Sun in Pisces, so we see with the Moon in this sign—a considerable sensitivity toward atmospheres and unconscious undercurrents of emotion in the immediate surroundings, toward which reactions are often made unconsciously. With the Moon there is this difference, however: the reactions have a background of the need for security (however unaware the natives may be of the fact!), whereas, with the Sun the background is the growth of the individuals' personal consiousness. Receptivity can sometimes render the native oversentimental.

The propensity for service inherent in the mutable cross makes those with Moon in Pisces suitable for various kinds of relief work (whether in a professional or lay capacity) provided their emotions are involved. People of this type will feel—without realizing it—the needs and wants of others and may well try to do something about them. Nevertheless, the double nature of the mutable cross does nothing to promote the emotional stability of the natives. They can toss to and fro in a rudderless fashion, at the mercy of impulses arising from the unconscious or from influences from outside. They find it difficult to tell the difference between the two, and, in fact, telling the difference will always give problems, even though experience will teach a great deal.

Individuals with the Moon in Pisces can sometimes appear to be very superficial in their reactions to the outside world. The mutable cross creates an impression of a lack of depth in spite of the presence of an intensely active emotional life. Because it *is* mutable, these natives find it hard to apply themselves steadily. The cause of this impression of superficiality may also be found in rather impersonal or collective behavior. What we then have is a poor sense of identity, and, without knowing it, these natives' first reaction is to tune in to the emotional program being beamed at them from the outside world and, in particular, to relay the emotions of the people with whom they happen to be at the time. The waves of emotion which they so readily pick up usually carry a message or opinion that is likely to be accepted as true. Later on they come back to their own opinion, or else someone arrives with another opinion which they may (without more ado) accept and follow. Those who have the Moon in Pisces are usually very compliant in all areas of life.

These natives' initial response to the outside world is passive, expectant, emotional and wary (water), yet they will quickly become involved, without realizing it, in anything touching their feelings.

The danger is that they will tend to lose their identity, although by being pliable they avoid problems when meeting people for the first time. Where they have difficulties is in forming opinions (when, for example, the rest of the horoscope points in the direction of a strong self-image).

The caring and cherishing characteristics, which also fall within the province of the Moon, are strongly developed in Pisces. These natives can enter into the feelings of others and can do everything possible to make others comfortable; they will knock on doors collecting for charity, and so on. Organizing this sort of thing suits Pisces individuals very well, whether they have the Sun or the Moon in the sign. That is to say, the mutable cross influence brings the inferior element air to the surface every now and then—in a way that does not always induce feelings of rest and harmony. Out of a dread of failing to achieve something, these natives indulge in "passionate logic" and in laying plans with feverish haste. Schemes, time schedules and work schedules are produced in order to insure the smooth running of whatever involves their emotions. But since the *inferior* element is at the bottom of all this, it is not a reliable character trait. Mental and rational activities can fall into abeyance for a long time while the natives trust to the guidance of their emotions entirely.

Due to the waiting attitude encouraged by the water element and to the dualism of the mutable cross, people with Moon in Pisces tend to be passive toward others. Often they copy what others are doing and look for some conscious or unconscious signal before they will act.

When in Pisces, the Moon creates the need to look for emotional security. The native is passively expectant and unconsciously assesses every situation in terms of emotions before determining a position. If the Pisces Moon comes across any impediments, it can become quickly withdrawn into a world of its own, full of sentiment, to which nobody else has access and where it can do and enjoy the things denied by reality. In a constructive sense this can lead to a richer inner life, which can find expression in music, poetry and other art forms. However, there may well be a tendency to various types of addiction or unhealthy habits. It is hard to say whether someone with Moon in Pisces will be led by a sense of insecurity to participate more eagerly in what is going on in the outside world. The fondness for inner experience is rather excessive, but the mutable cross makes it possible for the native to be outgoing—what will be done in practice will be suggested by the rest of the chart.

MERCURY IN PISCES

The urge to arrange, classify and analyze experience operates in Pisces in a manner that is hard to understand. In one respect it is purely emotional and subjective (water element influence), while in another respect it is dualistic (mutable cross). Therefore, there is a tendency to do without analyzing, arranging and assimilating—at least in the accepted sense of the words. Any arranging that is done follows illogical patterns, but the result can be as effective as a logical arrangement.

When in Pisces, Mercury often has more to do with the way in which individual facts and phenomena are seen. It operates here in an unstructured way, and is governed by the feelings and by a strong desire for change (mutable cross), which usually amounts to a quick succession of mental images and ideas. Hence, people with Mercury in Pisces are exceptionally imaginative and have a feeling for things which to others have no existence—such as sagas, myths and legends. They can use them as bearings to guide them through life. The truth and wisdom of fairy tales and myths is self-evident, and often they see nothing strange about believing in them.

The manner in which they communicate is reserved, quiet and passive and ruled by the feelings. They are full of understanding for others and can help people by talking to them, even though the informational content of what they say is low. What others find so helpful is a sympathetic manner. Now and then the mutability of the mutable cross gets the better of them in their relationship with the outside world and they lose that quiet and reserved way of speaking for the time being. But, in general, they "bottle up" this mutability inside, where it expresses itself in an enriched world of fantasy and imagery.

Like any other of the planets, Mercury is very impressionable when in Pisces. As a water sign, Pisces is naturally impressionable, but the mutable cross, which prompts continual adjustment and integration, also creates (in a very subtle manner) conditions which make the natives dependent on their environment. Therefore, the arranging, analyzing and combining of facts is done not only in an emotional and mostly subjective manner but, at the same time, in a manner that involves the outside world according to the sensitivity possessed by Mercury in this sign. This means that those with this placement of Mercury are much inclined to follow the ideas of people with whom they associate, and, without being aware of it or being able to resist it to any great extent, they can allow themselves to be drawn into things which can harm them although, if they are lucky, horizons may be expanded, giving them a deeper insight into life.

The inferior element, which may assert itself every now and again, will sometimes make these natives easily impressed by high-sounding logic and by all sorts of mental acrobatics being performed in the external world. They may have tremendous respect for people who can formulate thoughts clearly. Nevertheless, they will come to realize that with their emotional way of thinking, their liking for "proof by absurdity" and their roundabout methods of reasoning they can get as far, if not further, than others do. In other words, they are able to make use of dormant material which would never occur to the person of logic to employ and, by so doing, can come to terms with life in a different fashion. The sense of uncertainty imparted by having to live in a cerebral type of society may, however, make them feel inferior in this respect.

People with Mercury in Pisces tend to organize life around emotions, and emotions enter into thinking, speaking and communicating. They deploy other values than those supplied by logic—values imported from other dimensions. If thwarted, natives can ride hobbyhorses (due to emotional identification with certain ideas in which the inferior element can break through with an often primitive type of logic) or can withdraw into a dreamworld of fantasy. What they find in the latter may have little point of contact with reality, and yet owing to some strange power inherent in visions it may become reality every once in a while. Dreaming, and daydreaming too, can be very creative.

VENUS IN PISCES

The search for comfort and safety on emotional and material planes has an emotional background when Venus is in Pisces; what is more, the energy of the mutable cross makes its own contribution here, so the natives find it hard to say just what they are looking for.

The mutability implies a certain duality, and to some extent Venus shares in this duality when in Pisces. On the other hand, the need to become immersed and to integrate, to be of assistance and service, is also a property of the mutable cross, and can bring it about that people with Venus in Pisces will lose no time in looking for a relationship in which Venus can help in some way and can mean something to the other party, but can also become absorbed in the other. Perhaps it would be better to describe this as being integrated in the other person. The sense of identity of Venus in Pisces is not great and, because Venus is so easily influenced, it will be quickly inclined to follow the lead of the loved one or of the friends with whom Venus identifies. To become a veritable part of the other person is both significant and desirable to Venus in Pisces, not so much physically as spiritually: Venus needs to feel at one with friends or partner for a shared emotional experience. This need is often so great that the natives will pitch hopes too high and meet with disappointment; at least this is a distinct possibility when the rest of the horoscope indicates a lack of realism. Unfortunately, disappointment may incline Venus to reinforce the inner emotional life to the detriment of outer influences. A further result can be a burst of creativity, plus perhaps that consuming passion an artist feels for his/her work alone.

It is entirely possible that people with Venus in Pisces will want to experience a relationship as something straight out of a fantasy world; the imagination is certainly vivid enough for this. Indeed they may view life as a sort of opera in which friends and relatives make colorful entrances and exits and everything is musical and dramatic.

These natives' sensitiveness when striving for emotional security is very great and increases dependence on the partner. But there is a danger that they will become totally absorbed in a partner and will find it next to impossible to recover personal identity, or else will run into problems by regarding a partner as a kind of fairy-tale figure or by failing to establish a relationship with the partner as he or she really is. Such a state of affairs may even persist for a long time, since the mutable cross is not particularly helpful in getting to the heart of the problem to achieve a solution. Often the assuption is made that a difficulty has been resolved because it has been diagnosed. In truth, other factors are required for proper awareness; Venus in Pisces makes it hard for the individual to tell whether or not the fantasy world really exists, because Venus causes dreams to seem as palpable as the rest of experience.

Venus in Pisces naturally hovers in the region between reverie and reality and likes to idealize the partner. This is how Venus searches for comfort and safety on the emotional plane; it is also how Venus can involve itself in many disappointments, while yet experiencing things more intensely and more sweetly than many others do. Obstructions can never foil the search for an ideal, they can only push it more deeply into the inner life or else make the native seek compulsively for fulfillment in the outside world and make the ideal real in his or her own way.

MARS IN PISCES

A passive, impressionable attitude is the background to the working of Mars in Pisces, so that what the world at large sees in the native is slight activity and considerable quiescence and sloth. This appearance belies, however, an intense inner activity in the realm of dreams, fantasies and multifarious emotional processes. It is not easy for the world to recognize this activity, nor is it easy for the native to start putting it to good use.

At exit point the energy flow tends to become fragmented (mutable cross effect); also the main urge to action is emotional. There are some emotions which can arouse Mars from those (outwardly) Piscean slumbers. And, because Mars in Pisces is impressionable, other people also may manage by some means or other to stir the native into activity.

As the urge to stand apart and to assert oneself as a distinct personality, Mars encounters difficulties in Pisces; so what options are open to it in such a self-sacrificing, subservient and ultrasensitive sign? Well, when visiting this part of the zodiace, Mars can help people "born under him" to distinguish themselves from others by providing superior energy and enthusiasm in working for a good cause or for anything promoting the welfare of others. In this way Mars can sometimes get noticed; but, after toiling away patiently for a long time, Mars is quite capable of turning on companions for the "exploiting" that has taken place. Actually Mars here is fairly easily exploited due to an innate sensitivity and dependence.

Mars as the aggressive form of self-preservation hardly seems to know the meaning of self-preservation when in this sign. The native is open to subtle manipulation from outside and readily responds to atmospheres and waves of emotion. It is certainly possible for the instinct for self-preservation to express itself by resisting the spirit animating a certain place or gathering or by turning it to personal advantage, but, in general, Pisces has a damping effect on Mars. For want of freedom of expression, the martian energies tend to withdraw into the deeper regions of the psyche, to emerge only in case of extreme need; indeed, it is possible that the native's behavior may always remain dull and ineffectual simply because Pisces robs Mars of the weapons required to make its presence felt. If, however, there are indications of activity elsewhere in the horoscope, the native can be physically active even though the inner feelings mean the most. One likelihood, when physical activity and inner feelings combine, is a passion for music and dancing.

JUPITER IN PISCES

Jupiter, as the reflection of the need for spiritual values, for religious experience and for expansion in general, operates in an emotional manner Pisces. The Fishes, being an emotional sign and one easily influenced by the environment, will give shape to this need both spontaneously and via undercurrents in the surroundings (which may not be directly perceived by the native). Atmospheres and general moods can affect the way in which these needs work out. Thus Jupiter in Pisces, which can impart a feeling for universal values, can also bestow a liking for dogmas (especially if the inferior element air enters in) which may be adopted from some religious body. The native is more interested in content than in form.

Owing to the influence of the mutable cross, Jupiter in Pisces will experience considerable change, but this does not mean, for example, that the native will switch allegiance from one creed to another. The change may equally well consist of experiencing a great many religious and spiritual feelings which, through the image-building potential of Pisces, can be so powerful that a single faith or religious persuasion can supply more than enough impressions to keep the inner processes busy.

Because feelings are so easily aroused, but also because of an inclination to be somewhat impersonal, the native is readily caught up in any trend that takes the inner eye. Impersonality can arise from a lack of a sense of identity, but equally from the fact of reaching a stage of development in which the individual sees that ego forms a very small part of the psyche and that there is so much more in collective and universal values than in the value of an identity. From this vantage point the native can deploy a capacity for expansion completely unselfishly and disinterestedly, and so become a support and refuge for others.

Such compassion and the insight needed to sustain it is not yet available to the person who has so far failed to develop much of an identity (the first of the two alternatives mentioned in the previous paragraph). For this person, a creed, church or some other spiritual establishment lays a foundation for living on which he can build. At his particular stage of development, this can be just as important as analogous values (for example metaphysical values or experience of life) are for the person who has discovered the relativity of the ego.

The individual with Jupiter in Pisces will always wish to expand on the religious, spiritual and/or philosophical plane; he will desire to know himself and others and, if he can, to help them too. If the psychic energy is obstructed, its entire flow can be inward, so that the world observes little of his religious life; but then again, the native may feel impelled to reveal this inner life. Whatever may be the case, he needs to feel at one with all people, to feel (perhaps through some faith or metaphysical society) that in spite of external differences all people on Earth are one.

SATURN IN PISCES

The feelings play a large part in forming consciousness, but at the same time they are the weak point of anyone who has Saturn in Pisces. As in all the water signs, Saturn in this placement will try to protect itself against all kinds of emotional impacts and painful feelings by building a wall. The world cannot touch one here, but neither, after shutting oneself inside a personal igloo, can one share with the world the warmth one has to give. So, whereas the mutable cross influence in this water sign makes the native long for emotional variety, Saturn here quickly shuts out the emotional life. The native will soon realize how inadequate this reaction is, but the gravity of this does not dawn immediately. It can be quite a time before the native sees the isolation. Nevertheless, the mutable cross can set things in motion and solve the problems, provided, of course, the rest of the horoscope contains pointers in the same direction. Saturn by itself would make the native too nervous of the new to allow a breakthrough of the private wall of reserve.

The impersonality (in the sense of being subject to collective influences from outside) and the difficulty found by anyone under a strong Piscean influence of building up an identity, means that with Saturn in Pisces it will be very hard for the Saturnian potential to develop. What we mean by this is that it is Saturn's function to give shape to consciousness, and here Saturn has to operate in a sign that is retrospective, so that the native discovers who he is and signifies from what he sees he was not.

Learning through pain occurs here in the emotional life; the sense of responsibility is shaped by the feelings also. It will be clear that the person who has Saturn in Pisces can have a big sense of responsibility for certain things to which he is attached or for people who are dear to him, and he may sacrifice considerable time and effort in helping them.

In society at large, the native may suffer from identity problems or a feeling of worthlessness or failure. This can lead to psychosomatic disorder. In addition, his trouble gives him a ready excuse for failing to do as well as he should and he may well decide to make the most of it whenever he encounters some difficulty. This is an extreme result, but nevertheless it is a distinct possibility.

With an active inner life, a gift of imagination and the like, these people will also try to satisfy themselves with dreams and daydreams in order to compensate for falling short in everyday life. The result can be a sense of responsibility unrelated to reality or, if not unrelated, then wrongly related. Should these natives remain in this state of mind for too long and use it as a convenient escape route, they will lose perseverence and become reluctant to make decisions. They will let things drift while they are miles away in a fantasy world trying to find pseudosatisfaction. Therefore, people with Saturn in Pisces can go through life for a time in a sort of daze, until the Saturnian process of learning through pain has maneuvered them into an impossible situation where some extremely unpleasant predicament jolts them back to a sense of reality; then they have to begin all over again building up themselves and their position. Once they have come to themselves, they can turn to account the insight gained into the pitfalls and afflictions of life, and can do good in a quiet and often unassuming way (for example, in hospitals and similar institutions, by helping drug addicts or by working for Alcoholics Anonymous).

URANUS, NEPTUNE AND PLUTO IN PISCES

The urge to break the mold of form and to be original (Uranus), the need to refine form, to unravel it and to make it universal (Neptune), and the craving for power, confrontation and the transcendence of form (Pluto), will operate in a purely emotional manner in Pisces. In spite of the fact that the feelings may not display themselves in external form to any great extent, they can undergo considerable alterations owing to the influence of the mutable cross.

In the years between 1920 and 1928, Uranus transited Pisces and encouraged many changes in the undercurrents of emotional life. This may not have been immediately obvious in the new generation that was born under this influence, but the people who were children then are still hankering after all kinds of new emotional experience. In fact, at the time, the influence could be sensed rather than seen. These were the years after the First World War, which finally laid to rest the ghost of the nineteenth century and ushered in the spirit of the twentieth. The changes that had taken place in the unconscious mind of humanity paved the way for fresh attitudes and fresh values, and when Uranus entered Aries it had something new to contribute. Everything happened by fits and starts, but the generation with Uranus in Pisces is a very impressionable one, and apparently this is one of the strongest factors in the changes in values which have taken place after each of the world wars.

We shall have to wait until the twenty-first century before Neptune and Pluto enter Pisces, and Neptune will prepare the way for Pluto. Neptune will make human beings more responsive than ever to unconscious internal values—for other values than those affecting the ego. For Neptune this will be an entry into its own sign. But Pluto may ring in big chances, just as Uranus in Pisces has done in our own era. In matters like these, Pisces is the most significant of the signs: all is still unmanifest, but the seed has been sown. The manifestation of what is as yet unperceived occurs when the planet concerned crosses the cusp into Aries. Nevertheless, beginning and ending lie in Pisces.

Chapter Seven

A Closer Look at How the Planets Behave

1. Superior versus Inferior Element

In every horoscope you will find one or more planets placed in an element that does not belong to the element of consciousness, the superior element. This gives an extra dimension to the planets. In principle, their predisposing patterns are unchanged, but a few additional factors are introduced by this relationship with the role the planets play in the psyche as a whole. So we should never confine ourselves to studying the planets in the signs as such, but should work out the implications of the elements and crosses. The results can sometimes be quite surprising. For instance, planets which at a superficial glance appear to pose no problems (planets in their own signs, say, and without difficult aspects) can raise a whole series of problems when considered from another point of view. By way of illustration, it may be useful to review the theory of the elements and crosses as the basis of the horoscope as expounded in the first volume in this series.

We differentiate in the horoscope between an element that reveals the attitude of the conscious mind—the superior element— and an element situated in the unconscious mind—the inferior element, which, incidentally, is not inferior in quality but is out of the way of government and differentiation by the conscious. Each horoscope is subject to this tension. The conscious element, which can be identified with the help of a certain technique (see Volume I) can in fact be aided by the two remaining elements, which are neither superior nor inferior. These usually help the work of the conscious element, not as simultaneous developments, but one after the other. The inferior element always remains bound up with the unconscious. Now, if we discover an important factor in the inferior element, the predisposing pattern represented by this planet will also reveal certain unconscious characteristics. One of the most important of these is that someone with a given factor in the unconscious almost never feels at ease when this factor is at work inside. What is more, the factor is out of reach of the willpower of the individual, which is a feature of all unconscious factors. This person may become aware that certain unconscious reaction patterns are "programmed" within but may find it hard to understand them. They commonly take him by surprise, which can be disagreeable to the conscious mind, although he can also see them as reactions by which the unconscious keeps the conscious in check whenever the latter tends to become too one sided.

But however that may be, when we wish to examine the significance of the planets in the signs, we have to bear in mind the way in which the elements are disposed. This will show us where we may expect specific problems—and also where the native's potential lies.

To take an example: Let us suppose we have in front of us the birth chart of someone whose superior element is air. Air represents thinking, and it is through thinking that he will consciously approach the world, will experience and evaluate it. His inferior element, then, is water. Now, should Mercury be posited in the element water (for example, if the native is a Gemini with Mercury in Cancer), the planet will develop its activities down in the unconscious, which will make life difficult for this air type. What we mean by this is that Mercury is a naturally objective planet and represents the faculty in man that inclines him to arrange, to analyze and to make associations as neutrally and as objectively as possible. However, a planet that exerts its influence from the unconscious part of the mind can hardly be called objective: it is colored by all kinds of personal, repressed and collective materials. And although the collective unconscious can display unprecedented objectivity (as in our dreams!), there remains a gulf between the inferior factors and the way in which they are interpreted by the superior element. The unconscious factors express themselves in a symbolic language that the conscious mind often finds puzzling and may misread.

Thus, when Mercury is acting out of the inferior element and when, as in our example, this element is water, the planet will lose its neutrality and will encourage a manner of ordering, thinking, and analyzing which is strongly colored by the emotions. If this is pointed out, the native will probably hasten to deny it. His nature (here that of Gemini) invariably favors maximum objectivity (since he readily identifies with his Sun sign) and he imagines, in a *sub*jective way, that he is extremely *ob*jective in the manner in which he classifies and analyzes the things he is thinking about. When it is a factor in the inferior element, Mercury is deprived of its power of judgment. Only as life goes on will the native gradually come to a faint realization that something is "wrong." Such a situation need not be altogether disadvantageous; indeed he may well benefit from it. For, clearly, the thinker who ignores his emotional life may become one-sided and so strictly abstract as to be somewhat empty; but, if he has Mercury in water as his inferior element, he can keep a loophole open for his feelings. They may perhaps trouble him (making him rather insecure), but that need not always give rise to difficulties. By trying to fathom the various feelings of insecurity within he can get to the bottom of a number of problems. Also, he can understand others better when he is prepared to recognize that, via the conflict between thinking (air) and feeling (water), he himself is in search of alternative values and concepts.

If, however, he denies that he has a problem (which might best be thought of as a kind of "creative frustration"), he can land himself in overcompensation. He may, for instance, parade his "objectivity," may refuse to allow any criticism of his ideas (Mercury in an inferior element is very sensitive to criticism) and can ride hobbyhorses.

Mercury in Cancer does not mean the same thing in every horoscope without exception. The danger of becoming obsessed with some pet idea is greatly reduced in another combination of planets in which Mercury forms *no* part of the inferior element. This means that when judging the planets in the signs we have to take into account individual combinations and configurations in the horoscope.

Planets posited in the superior element are likely to develop their influences according to the usual patterns. As far as the planets up to and including Saturn are concerned, they have fairly free play in the conscious life of the individual. On the other hand, planets posited in the inferior element work in ways which prove awkward and incomprehensible to the conscious mind. Generally speaking, they display the following characteristics:

a) often they are somewhat slow in their development;

b) their influence tends to surface at unexpected moments and in unlooked for ways which can prove to be upsetting at times;

c) they can make the native unsure of himself in the areas ruled by them; so that, for example, he will brook no criticism of his behavior in those areas or will miss the point of certain observations others make concerning those areas;

d) they give a penchant for executing feints and a proneness to overcompensate, so that those around do not always know what to expect next.

A good example of the effect of such a planet is an inferior element is the planet Venus in Fred's horoscope on page 174. His superior element is earth, immediately followed by the element water as an auxiliary function. Therefore, the elements fire and air are unconscious. Fire is his inferior element, and air acts out of the unconscious, too, as a mainly inferior element, although there is some chance that Fred will later be able to integrate that element in his life to some extent. Venus, being in the inferior element air (the sign Gemini), operates in an inferior way, and this suggests that there may have been problems with the opposite sex. Venus in Gemini is already in a certain amount of trouble when it comes to forming a deep relationship. The danger is that the relationship will remain at a superficial level for a long time, although offsetting this is the fact that Fred, as a Taurus with a Scorpio Ascendant, is strongly attached to the partner and wants nothing better than to experience a deep and lasting relationship. Fred recalled that he had a girlfriend years ago but was never completely sure whether he was in love with her or not. He experienced great difficulty with the "conscious" expression of his Venus factor, and his girlfriend used to make him even more unsure by asking him whether or not he really loved her. If Venus had been in an earth or in a water sign his problems would have been far less, regardless of the way in which the planet exerted its influence. Venus in Capricorn, say, can make the native too cool and unemotional in his dealings with others, but this placement would have created fewer problems for Fred than does Venus in Gemini. Of course, it goes without saying that not everyone with Venus in Gemini will encounter the same difficulties. We must always look at the position taken up by Venus in relation to the other factors in the scheme of the elements.

In spite of the fact that a planet in an inferior element can go hand in hand with uncertainty and difficulties, it is also an intermediary that brings us into contact with our unconscious. This same position in Fred's chart is a stimulus for him in order to express the strong Venusian feelings he finds so hard to handle—but on another plane. His Moon in Pisces helps him here, and with this combination he can discharge a great deal of feeling in making music, say, and can also find much satisfaction in the practice and appreciation of music and art. As a Sun in Taurus/Moon in Pisces the native already has a feeling for these things; the emotional tension bestowed by the planet Venus is an added stimulus. In many horoscopes there are certain points of action. However, exactly *what* is done with the energy they supply has to be deduced from the relationship of the planet concerned with other factors in the chart. A planet in a sign never stands or falls by itself.

2. FAVORABLE AND ADVERSE EFFECTS OF VARIOUS PLANETARY PLACEMENTS

Closely linked with what has been said in the foregoing paragraph is the question of to what extent given planetary positions support or hinder one another. Some planets, by their placement, can be either boosters or brakes to another planet in the same or in another sign without there having to be any disharmony between the elements. People often think that if a certain planetary placement implies an influence that conflicts with that of another the two tend to cancel each other out, so that they lose at least something of their effect. Nothing could be further from the truth! When we have two conflicting factors, the conflict will reveal itself in the character of the person concerned. This can happen in any number of ways: sometimes one factor and sometimes the other will gain the upper hand. Should one factor reign supreme, the other will be suppressed, causing either severe internal struggle or much uncertainty on that point. In some respects, the contest between the two factors can play a very important role. In order to see how the above situation might work out in everyday life, let us take a look at the following example. Suppose Jupiter and Saturn are in the same sign without being in conjunction and therefore not aspecting one another. Because these incompatible predisposing factors are expressing themselves in the same fashion (the same sign), they do have something to do with one another and can influence each other accordingly. Jupiter represents the human need for religious and spiritual values, the need for expansion, for insight and understanding. The Jupiter nature wants to view everything in a wide setting and to experience a synthesis. How different is Saturn—the process of learning through pain! This is the factor that has to do with the formation of consciousness, with coming to know one's limitations. At the same time it is a sensitive spot. We shape ourselves through Saturn; often through taking some pretty hard knocks. Therefore is the planet so frequently associated with fear, inhibitions and overcompensation.

When the two factors are in the same sign, the way in which they operate is the same. Pain (Saturn) and healing power (Jupiter) go together. A person whose chart has Saturn in Virgo (element earth) is likely—because of Virgo's sociable mutability—to feel the urge to serve others in a concrete and practical way (apart from other features in the horoscope which we shall leave out of consideration for the sake of simplicity). Saturn in Virgo gives, on the one hand, an exaggerated desire to be helpful (overcompensation) or, on the other, the impulse to hedge offers of help with all kinds of restrictions. Mental analysis, too, is concrete and thorough, but anxieties and inhibitions may mean that others, if not the native himself (as sometimes happens), are put under the magnifying glass. Saturn in Virgo, then, wavers between giving as much help and sympathy as possible and the fear of becoming too deeply involved.

With Jupiter in Virgo, inner growth can take place in a Virgoan manner, so that the observation and analysis of facts and meditation on them lead to insights into self and others. There are no limitations here as there are with Saturn. The expansion of Jupiter does not take place along broad lines, however, since that is not possible in a sign like Virgo. Attention is paid to detail, obligation, and service (earth and the mutable cross). The individual with Jupiter in Virgo needs to help others in order to be able to help himself, and needs to analyze himself and others minutely in order to gain a better insight into himself and into his role in society or, indeed, in life itself. Hence, we see that the thing that can help a person to make life pleasant (Jupiter), to improve his lot and to come to grips with essentials may need help in developing a clearly defined awareness of what he is trying to attain (Saturn). In itself, this is probably a good thing but, remember, Saturn is also the sensitive point, the difficult factor in the horoscope and, whenever Jupiter sets out full of enthusiasm, Saturn raises fears, doubts, uncertainty and hesitation. Therefore, the native may let opportunities slip through his fingers from time to time. On the other hand, when Saturn inclines the native to overcompensate and to prove that he is neither afraid nor vulnerable, Jupiter can push him even further in the same direction so that the overcompensation is augmented.

Nevertheless, there are easier sides to this planetary combination. For instance, when Saturn drags the native down in the dumps and he sits there in a state of depression, Jupiter can lift him out of it. Jupiter's cheery message is "broadcast on the same wavelength" as Saturn's more somber one and, no matter how deep the Saturnian influence goes, the comforting power of Jupiter can put the native on top of the world again.

Let us assume, for instance, that the individual with Saturn in Virgo has been working full steam in fulfillment of some promise of assistance. He is tense and suspects that he is not being appreciated for his efforts. Jupiter, working out of the same background, can find some enjoyment in being helpful because this can be used as an instrument for inner growth. The satisfaction of a good job done, whether thanks are received for it or not, is enough for Jupiter to mitigate the dejection or melancholy of Saturn.

When Jupiter and Saturn are in the same sign, one or other of the following results may be anticipated:

a) Saturn inhibits Jupiter from fully expressing its possibilities;

b) Jupiter is able to lift Saturn out of its low point;

c) when both factors are activated simultaneously, overcaution can mean missed chances;

d) Jupiter can confirm Saturn's overcompensations; but

e) Jupiter can also give the native an insight into the way in which Saturn is making him overcompensate and can weaken his tendency to do so;

f) both factors can strengthen or weaken each other;

g) the native's character can go to extremes due to these strengthening or weakening influences.

To the extent that the confrontations are experienced through the character, the process of assimilation can do its work. If the native manages to give gradual shape to the Saturnian influence (for example, by learning how to overcome the anxiety produced by the planet), the latter can in increasing measure lend depth and perseverance to the other factor in this sign, Jupiter. But the road is a long one. Yet, Saturn and Jupiter in the same sign are able to form the character in such a way that blame and shame, pain and hardship (Saturn), lead to wisdom—a wisdom (Jupiter) to be shared by others as the native renders them assistance in a truer, wider and more comprehensive way.

The above illustration of two conflicting factors makes it clear that as far as the planets in the signs are concerned we have to pay due attention to the kind of duality described above. Such dualities will never be resolved; their components are equally and untiringly active, and they interplay incessantly. The problems arising here are completely different from those involved in the partition of the elements. It should be obvious that when Saturn and Jupiter are shedding their influence from the same sign, the result will be entirely different when we are dealing with the superior element from what it is when we are dealing with the inferior element. These may appear to be small points but, nevertheless, they are extremely important if we wish to understand why identical factors in two horoscopes seem to work out dissimilarly.

3. WHAT ELSE CAN WE DO WITH THE PLANETS?

A knowledge of the general significance of the planets in a horoscope is usually insufficiently informative and the question is often raised as to what can be done with these basic meanings. It is incorrect to imagine that if we try to do our best in life, difficult factors will automatically vanish, never to return. Life is ever changing and its shifting scenes keep demanding from us new ways of adjustment and growth. Nothing stays as it is, and the inner self makes fresh demands as one stage of life succeeds another. Even if we have managed to overcome or to evade a problem in one phase, it can raise its ugly head again in a different guise in another phase or in other circumstances. We play at hide-and-seek with ourselves more often than we would care to admit, and find that a factor we thought we had dodged will come swaggering up to us in camouflage. The "new" old difficulty requires a new and different solution, and problems will still keep budding from one and the same planetary position until we get to the root of the situation. Once we have come to know the root cause apart from all external manifestations, we shall have in our hands a key to improvement. Admittedly, the factor will always be with us, but an influence that creates difficulties can be taken and made to work positively!

An example will serve us here. Due to a certain planetary constellation and a certain predisposing pattern, Rob developed a mother complex very early in life. There was a strong bond with his mother, and he was the apple of her eye. When they started to have differences of opinion, Rob took it into his head that being tied to his mother's apron strings was spoiling his prospects, even though she actively encouraged his social life. Anyway, something seemed to be wrong somewhere, so he broke off contact with her in order to "be his own man" and, for a while, felt a great sense of relief, believing that he had solved all his problems and was now ready to forge ahead. However, he was reckoning without considering the inner yearnings represented by that troublesome planetary constellation.

Not long after "gaining his freedom" he fell under the spell of an experienced older woman who, as a lover, was able to exercise a more than motherly control over him. It was not a smooth relationship. He was hoping to preserve some semblance of independence and tried to drag his heels over some of the things she wanted him to do, but he soon found that she was the dominant partner and was going to make him do them in spite of any protests. She took the line that as "her little boy" she knew what was best for him and that he must not be allowed to have his own way. In the end, his ardor for her cooled and he left her—again with a sigh of relief—before she had finished taming him!

Next he threw himself heart and soul into his work and concentrated on pushing himself—to such an extent that he suffered from overstrain. He accused his work for his breakdown, even though it had recently meant so much to him, and wanted to change jobs. Then he remembered how strictly he had been brought up and how his mother had instilled into him that "idleness is the Devil's" and hard work a virtue. Suddenly it dawned on him that his rupture with his mother had been futile since his mind was still under her influence. His stint of hard work had been a response to her conditioning, and he had been looking for her guiding hand when he became infatuated with his bossy lady friend.

Gradually Rob began to identify the components in his makeup which gave him a weakness for petticoat government, especially when it was exercised by an older woman. He ceased to place the entire blame for his hang-ups on others. Perhaps as he gains a more balanced approach to life, he may be able to cope with the difficult planetary constellation. He needs a safety valve for the feelings associated with the latter. Such a safety valve could release considerable creativity.

We stand a better chance of seeing where various problems lie if we study the background of certain planets in the signs than we do if we view the forms of expression purely in the concrete plane. For example, Mars can generate a great deal of aggression whether posited in Aries or Scorpio. The planet is the same but the background is not; the aggression in the first case will have a different cause from what it has in the second. If we hope to understand and cope with aggression, we must discover its exact cause. The individual with Mars in Aries may become pugnacious because of excess energy which he is unable to discharge quietly at a certain moment or for which he is unable to find fresh outlets— a situation he finds hard to tolerate. The best way to deal with an aggressive child with Mars in Aries is to let him engage in pleasurable activities such as sports. The child with Mars in Scorpio, on the other hand, feels a surge of aggression rising up inside him whenever his insecurity becomes too great. Mars in Scorpio can give rise to all sorts of overcompensation. So this child is not in urgent need of letting off steam like the child with Mars in Aries. Instead he needs to be occupied with something which will reassure him and build up his self-confidence. Certainly, some form of sport might serve this purpose, but the physical aspect is not so important here since the aggression is not an overspill of energy unable to find a natural outlet.

Equally as important as the background factors associated with a certain planet in a sign is the particular cross to which the sign belongs. Forgetting for a moment the business of inferior and superior elements, let us pay attention to the assimilatory processes represented by the three crosses. Thus the cardinal cross type can assimilate experience by means of the external world and the part he plays in it. This certainly does not mean that he need never retire into himself in order to work things out. He will in fact do so from time to time even without problems to prompt him. For this purpose it is best if there is a planet in a fixed sign in his birth chart, capable of confronting him with the deeper layers of his being and thus with his inferior element. Then he will be able to occupy himself in a manner and on a plane suggested by the planet in the sign (the sign itself indicating the mode of assimilation). We must not assume, however, that he can identify himself permanently with the given planet, and even less that he will suddenly change his characteristic mode of assimilation, attitude to life or approach to a specific problem. All that will happen is that, by accepting the influence of the said planet in the said sign, he will find the corresponding mode of assimilation activated in him.

Most people will, from time to time, quite spontaneously endeavor to enter the territory of a planet. The planet that attracts them there represents a natural need; however, we do find people who, for some reason or other, hesitate to enter it although, as they have discovered, doing so supplies a lack. The cross in which the planet stands represents an auxiliary mode of assimilation. So—to take the fixed cross for instance—one man will find himself more easily through Mercury (by arranging, classifying, analyzing and so on) while another will seek a confrontation with his unconscious through Mars (action, self-assertion and so on). Thus, everyone has one or more planets making a certain mode of assimilation available to him. This applies even to the transsaturnian planets.

If someone is badly off balance, and if he has one or more planets in mutable signs, help is at hand to restore equilibrium (the mutable cross assimilates by harmonizing, serving, etc.) regardless of the nature of the planets. Say the planet in question is Uranus; then, surprising as it might seem to others, the individual could recover balance by asserting independence, trying to be original or even by being downright provocative! Activities in which normal boundaries are crossed, such as cartomancy, astrology, occultism in general, or maybe aviation and telecommunications, are other possible forms of expression by which he can get himself together again. A single planetary pattern has many possible ways of expressing itself, the above-mentioned are only a few. Uranus, being an explosive influence, can even restore the equilibrium by some form of breakage—quite literally. Thus, an exasperated lady may find relief in smashing a once favorite tea-set to smithereens. We may rest assured that the energy will express itself in one way or another. By studying the crosses we can arrive at a better understanding of ourselves, and of what factors will help us in our contacts with others (cardinal cross planets) and what will help to redress the balance between our conscious and our unconscious (mutable cross planets). The particular elements involved will then give us a decisive answer on the question of the extent to which we are able to use a given planet's influence consciously—or the extent to which the predisposing pattern will be experienced apart from our conscious minds.

One last point on superior and inferior effects: take the horoscope of someone who clearly has the element air as the superior element but also has the Moon in Scorpio. With the Moon posited in Scorpio, the fixed cross is liable to bring the inferior element—in this case air—into the open. It is tempting to say that air is already superior and that therefore the Moon in Scorpio has nothing to do with inferior factors. But that is precisely what we must never do! In a fixed water sign (Scorpio) the Moon is characterized by being primarily oriented to the feelings, and although the "thinking impulse" can show itself from time to time, it will obviously be inferior as far as the Moon in a water sign is concerned. It will never be able to thrust aside the emotional behavior of the Moon. Nevertheless, as soon as the thought processes get under way, the native's psyche will switch over to the air element—the superior function—automatically, and some planet other than the Moon will predominate while the Moon itself most likely goes out of play. Hence we can make the following statements:

a) A planet in a fixed sign will always dredge up from the unconscious mind certain factors bearing the impress of the inferior element. For example: the Sun in Taurus (earth) will haul inferior fire to the surface. The Moon in Scorpio (water) brings out inferior air. *This relationship between superior and inferior goes with the placement of the planet in the sign.*

b) Likewise, a planet in a mutable sign, albeit to a lesser extent, will occasionally bring unconscious, inferior factors into the open.

c) When the distribution of the elements in a person's birth chart shows that the element air, say, is the element of consciousness, in other words is the superior element, planets in water signs will be influencing from the unconscious.

d) If a person has Moon in Scorpio, this Moon will operate from the unconscious, that is to say in an inferior mode. However, with Moon in Scorpio, the fixed cross brings factors out of the unconscious from what is (for *this* Moon) the inferior element air. This will also shed its influence from the unconscious and will remain inferior, in spite of the fact that other factors in *air* signs will work in a superior way for this native.

The planets in the signs can be a key to self-knowledge, but in spite of the important role they form only a part of the total interpretation of the birth chart. The houses and aspects provide further information and possibilities of refinement; they reveal how much support and inhibition are contained in the forms of expression of the planets. They show how their influences can develop and to which aspects of life they will apply. But the elements and crosses in the signs do intervene from their background position and give the way in which the predisposing patterns tend to manifest.

Two Example Horoscopes

1. Introduction

We shall now take a closer look at the predisposing patterns and the possible forms of expression in a chart. This can be no more than one part of horoscope interpretation for there are many other factors of importance which will come up for discussion in the next two volumes in this series.

The horoscopes discussed in the following paragraphs are mainly intended as practice, so that the reader can test what he or she has learned so far. These charts were also used as example in Volume 1 of this series.

2. Fred's Horoscope

Fred's Sun is in Taurus, as are his Mars and his Mercury. (See Chart 1 on page 174.) With three personal factors in one sign, we may safely place strong emphasis on that sign. Fred will always give priority to building material security and to clinging to concrete reality. He feels most at ease by so doing (Sun), and this is the background to the way in which he analyzes and makes connections between people and events (Mercury). His thinking will always start with what he considers to be essential, without giving it a second thought: solid fact. He likes to confine his attention to the tangible, to the tried and trusted. The experience he acquires is arranged

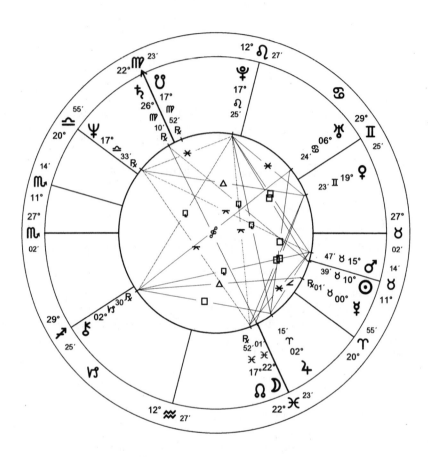

Chart 1. Fred's chart. He was born on May 1, 1951, in Gronigen, Holland, at 9:30 PM. The time is from his birth certificate. House system is Placidus. Chart used with permission.

according to known and perceptible patterns; everything is reduced to what can be seen or touched (Mercury in Taurus). He can really identify himself with this manner of arranging and analyzing (the Sun in the same sign).

Since the Taurean mode of assimilation is "slow but sure," the way in which the native orders and analyzes his experiences is also thorough and deliberate. Therefore, Fred will not react quickly to anything involving essential matters, even though with Venus in Gemini he can often seem bright and breezy in social life.

The fixed cross (to which Taurus belongs) brings it about that (with Mercury in the sign) he will talk in a calm and level-headed way and will reflect well before making important decisions. He likes to be sure of what he says. He tries to preserve this calm and measured approach because his need for certainty applies to his Sun, Mercury and Mars, and each of them supports the others in it.

His response to the external world, especially in situations he finds uncertain, is that of the Moon in Pisces: emotional and sensitive. He can detect atmospheres and undercurrents, but his Mercury in Taurus will translate them into concrete terms as quickly as possible. Due to the mutability of the Moon in Pisces, his initial reaction is to display some helpfulness—really with the aim of creating a secure position for himself. On the other hand, the duality of the Moon in Pisces adds uncertainty to his search for security. But, since he is a Sun sign Taurus native, little of this uncertainty will apear on the outside or in his contacts (Mercury in Taurus). He "chews the cud" first.

So, his first reaction is inward, while outwardly he remains passive and cautiously observant, due to the Pisces Moon. This is not to say that Fred will always hold his tongue. He is likely to be a bright conversationalist in company (Venus in Gemini), but that is a form of behavior that he can use to mask his real feelings while he is passing through a phase of insecurity. Once he has found security in the emotional sphere, Moon in Pisces and the fixity of Taurus will make him loathe to leave it. Hence, he can form a loyal emotional union with certain individuals. If anything happens to disturb this union, he will be thrown more off balance than he will care to admit.

Emotional matters of this kind are not always easy for him to handle; they are imponderable. With Mercury in Taurus, he will look for ways and means of making them tangible. His best opportunities in this direction lie in whatever appeals to the senses—music, are and the like—and he does possess the faculties to participate in and enjoy them.

His Mars works in the same direction. Considerable energy (Mars) is drawn inward (fixed cross) and invested in unconscious processes. The aggression which can be associated with Mars may not show up on the outside to begin with, but it certainly does a great deal in Fred himself: his inner life is more intense than would appear on the surface (this, too, in combination with Moon in Pisces). But when Fred moves to action, it will be due to some concrete need, and he will prefer to operate on the concrete plane by working with something tangible (mainly owing to the combination of the Sun in Mercury in the same sign). He is persevering, hard working and pushes himself when necessary (Mars in a fixed sign); his perseverance receives further emphasis from Sun and Mercury in Taurus. The perseverance will show itself both internally (he will turn things over in his mind for a long time) and externally (he is content to occupy himself with concrete matters indefinitely). When he lays down his tools we can be sure that, with Mars in Taurus, he is really (Sun in Taurus) through using them.

Fred has a placement of Venus that seems difficult to reconcile with the picture we have built up so far. Venus (the need for emotional security) is in Gemini—a mental and very mutable sign—and is always a bright and breezy factor with very little understanding of this same emotional security. It is so at variance with the other factors in his makeup that Fred hardly knows what to make of it. He will gradually come to realize that he has something in him somewhere that will enable him to take life more easily than he thought he could. Venus in Gemini makes him fond of change in affairs of the heart, but in favor of a union of like minds: he will want a partner he can talk to. However, Fred's Moon in Pisces pulls him in an opposite direction and calls for a partner with whom he can experience an emotional union that offers security. Thus, the Moon and Venus will make Fred hanker after two completely different things, and the mutability of their respective signs (Gemini and Pisces) contributes little to the stability of these needs. In fact, he will spend a good part of his life sorting out what his emotional needs really are. Since the Sun in Taurus is security minded, this is a more important matter than might be expected from the positions of the Moon and Venus alone.

By looking at the foregoing in the light of the distribution of the elements (See Vol. 1, p. 17), we can extract further information on the effect of Venus in Gemini. As a planet in an unconscious element (air is here the second ancillary function, water is obviously the first; usually the second ancillary function develops later, and sometimes not at all), Venus will itself operate from the region of the unconscious with the inevitable consequences of that. Fred's conscious mind has no handle on it. He may experience the factor as something outside "himself" and this can contribute to his uncertainty. All this means that his need for emotional security and his need for secure relationships are always hovering in the background, and make themselves felt at unexpected and possibly inconvenient moments. Thus, as a Taurean with Moon in Pisces, he favors a quiet retiring life, but every now and then his Venus in Gemini will make him hanker after contacts and changes of scene, and this he finds hard to cope with. So, Venus in Gemini is a disturbing factor in this otherwise rather stolid horoscope.

Venus in Gemini can make the native mercurial in company. Venus is the hand held out to give and to receive warmth, and since this factor in Fred's chart is an unconscious one, he can find it rather baffling. Yet he will, from time to time, be able to use a light and airy approach that will help him in contacts with others, especially as his verbal ability (Mercury) is not so fluent when it comes to essentials, and his Moon in Pisces is not particularly confident in making contacts. Venus, the planet of social contacts, can then break through, and so to speak, confront him with a breezy, intellectual, cordial and cheerful part of himself that makes a pleasant contrast with the more sober side of his character, even though he cannot understand what is making him so bright and talkative (it comes from his unconscious) and sometimes fears he may be making a fool of himself (since this is not behavior that the Moon in Pisces finds comfortable).

And so Venus in Gemini seems, on the one hand, to prevent Fred from becoming too reserved, though, on the other hand it is a factor that tends to make him feel lonely—however contradictory this may sound. He will have his more frivolous moments, but for the most part he will be fairly melancholy, sensitive and serious (as the rest of his personality demands). To prevent him from becoming isolated, the influence of Venus in Gemini can, quite apart from any conscious intention on his part, give him many contacts in the outer world. Nevertheless, he will have the uncomfortable feeling that these friends do not see him as he really is, and he has difficulty maintaining his false image.

These crosscurrents are the more significant because Venus, the ruler of Taurus, is in Gemini, while Mercury, the ruler of Gemini, is in Taurus. The two psychic influences are continually supplying one another with feedback.

Since all the factors endeavor to objectify themselves and must not be thought of as cancelling one another out, Fred suffers from emotional unrest both internally and in his relationships with women. The Moon and Venus in a man's horoscope partly represent the way he is treated by women and what he (unconsciously) expects of them.

Finally, Jupiter and Saturn, factors which do not exert quite such a pronounced effect on the personality and yet add a wholly individual dimension to the horoscope, complete the picture as follows. Jupiter as the spiritual and religious needs, and also the need for expansion and improvement, sheds its influence from Aries—from Fred's inferior element. The fixed cross of his Sun sign (Taurus) will keep bringing to the surface the element fire to some extent, and with it the subsidiary factor—Jupiter with its urge to remove old boundaries and comfortable limitations. When in Aries, Jupiter can do this in a fairly surprising manner, but the powerful fixed cross (with the Sun, Mercury and Mars among others) will have a certain inhibiting effect. Somewhere deep inside him there is an urge for expansion which he does not understand. Like Venus, Jupiter operates unconsciously. However, he cannot deny this factor; it is able to draw him out of his shell and can let him see more sides of the world, both literally and metaphorically. Essentially, though, it can undermine his conscious mind. His need for security and for safe, fixed borders—both internally and externally (Taurus again!)—can be badly shaken when Jupiter in Aries really "cuts loose," as is quite likely to happen at times because Aries is a cardinal sign encouraging expression in the outside world.

The need to enjoy life (Sun in Taurus) is given a somewhat adventurous cast by Jupiter in Aries, which can simmer for a long time inwardly, but can also manifest on the concrete plane— although Saturn in Virgo will act as a delay threshold. Fred has a great feeling of responsibility about material things (Virgo is a earth sign) and Saturn in Virgo makes him vulnerable on this very plane where his great strength lies. Because of its vulnerability, Saturn in a earth sign will incline him to safeguard his interests as much as possible. Fred's Sun strengthens the need for material security.

The mutability and desire to be of service inherent in Virgo means that although Fred (with Jupiter in Aries) may secretly dream of all sorts of adventures (prompted by the imaginative faculty of Moon in Pisces), his main interest is to achieve in everyday life the material security of which we have been speaking. This is not due to childishness, as is the case with some fire sign natives who like to set out haphazard. Fred's whole pattern of behavior flows from an inner drive to which Saturn in Virgo makes a considerable contribution. For owing to his need to be useful, both to himself and others, and to make an exact analysis of and to ruminate on everything and everybody (Saturn in combination with his Mercury in Taurus), he ventures into new situations tardily or, if possible, avoids them altogether. Nor will he start promoting his own interests until he has fulfilled all his obilgations. Even then he will want to make himself useful in some other way. His character is formed by Saturn in Virgo and he has an essential need to serve others. Since Saturn is making itself felt from his superior element and is linked with his Sun in Taurus, it is able to develop a powerful influence on the conscious mind of the native of this horoscope, quite apart from the aspects and houses involved.

3. PETER'S HOROSCOPE

Peter's horoscope, Chart 2 on page 180, is quite different from Fred's. The Sun is in Aries, a fire sign, which gives Peter the need to plunge into life in an enthusiastic, vivacious and "fiery" manner. The cardinal cross inclines him to go out into the world or, at any rate, to make his mark in his neighborhood. Nevertheless, in spite of his strong involvement with himself as a fire sign native, he is to some extent dependent on the world around him. This is because, as a member of a cardinal sign, he requires all kinds of impulses to keep him busy and to occupy his mind.

His Moon in Taurus plays him false however. In order to feel emotionally secure, Peter needs to have material protection that his other side (Sun in Aries) finds incomprehensible. Even as a child, Peter must have experienced an internal duality. On the one hand he could hear the alluring call of the wide world; on the other, he was led by Moon in Taurus to desire the safety of a comfortable home.

He is not likely to say much about his inner duality. Mercury is in Pisces, so it will not be easy for him to get the various factors within into any sort of order, not will it be easy for him to discuss his

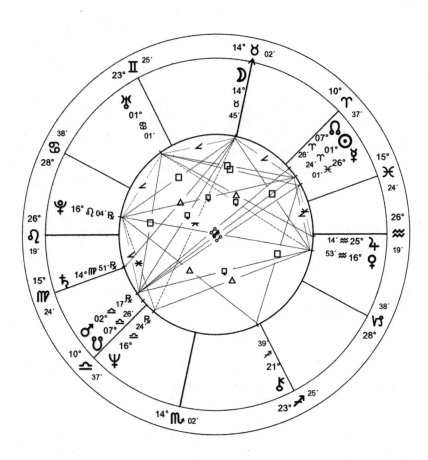

Chart 2. Peter's chart. He was born on March 22, 1950, at Lisse, Holland, at 3:30 PM. The data is supplied from his birth certificate. House system is Placidus. Chart used with permission.

problems. What this placement of Mercury does mean is that he will evaluate his experiences on an emotional basis, forgetting what he no longer wishes to know, dreaming of what he would like to do, but mostly keeping his thoughts to himself. He has great powers of imagination, something his Sun in Aries can support because it encourages whatever is new and adventurous. His imagination enables him to run through all sorts of "adventures" in his head without having to forego any creature comforts (Moon in Taurus). To some extent he will need to enjoy a life of daydreams but will also feel the attraction of the world around him bustling with new activities and full of new things. It is not altogether easy to come to terms with this situation, and it is likely that, unless their acquaintanceship with Peter is of many years standing, many of his friends will not know what to make of him. Even he will find it hard to decide what he really wants to do in the light of his conflicting impulses.

The whole thing is made more difficult by the fact that the Sun and the Moon stand in two opposing elements. Certainly, when he is young, the Sun represents the superior part of his psyche, so that in this case the Moon sheds its influence from the unconscious. He will be all too ready to deny the need for comfort and safety, for security and material wealth, which he definitely possesses; but that is only natural, since with his Sun in Aries, a cardinal sign, he is hardly orientated toward his unconscious. All covert actions to make himself comfortable are in stark contrast to a conscious attitude of "let's enjoy life while we may" (Sun in Aries).

The fire-earth duality created by the positions of his Sun and Moon places him in a degree of difficulty as far as material things are concerned. Not that he is unable to manage them but that the unconscious part of his mind is involved in the process. The presence of the Moon in Taurus in the inferior part of his psyche causes him to attend to his material needs by fits and starts. For his own part, this does not bother him, but problems arise when by mismanagement he allows things to get in a muddle, an event which is highly likely since Saturn, the factor representing a sense of responsibility, operates from his inferior element (earth), certainly in his younger years.

Due to his Sun being in Aries and his Moon being in Taurus, Peter is torn between the need for freedom and opportunity and the need for comfort and safety. This duality that sometimes seems so fickle to the outside world receives small comfort from two other personality factors, Venus and Mars.

Venus in Aquarius gives Peter the need for friends with whom he can talk, friends who will share the same vision with him and with whom he can feel at one. Conversation itself, represented by Mercury in Pisces, flows easily only when he is with a congenial group of friends. The atmosphere in which conversations are conducted is very important, thanks to Mercury in Pisces; but Venus in Aquarius also has a say in this matter. Venus in a fixed sign can increase the sensitivity to atmospheres. The inferior side of Venus in Aquarius (an air sign) is always water, the element in which Peter's Mercury is posited. This means that on the one hand Venus gives Peter a need for a good mental contact with friends, and especially with his partner, but that conversation gets going only when the atmosphere is not intellectual but emotional (the emotional charge is generated by Venus in the unconscious, from which it is released by the fixed cross). If the "vibes" are good, Peter (with Mercury in Pisces) can express himself well and will lose his reserve.

Because Venus in Aquarius is in a fixed sign, Peter can keep certain ideas and opinions to himself for a long time, although the need to communicate typical of an air sign demands a degree of openness. With his Venus in Aquarius, Peter can be very tolerant toward those who think differently from himself, but on certain points he is usually convinced that he is in the right, or so it *seems*. For with his Mercury in Pisces he is sensitive to all sorts of undercurrents, which can gradually and imperceptibly carry him in the direction of other notions and opinions. He is very susceptible to manipulation under the surface although, as an Aries, he thinks he is not. However, once he is taken with some newly formed idea, he can stick with it for a long time.

Mars in Libra also gives a need for contacts; he likes to be with people and to play an active part in his neighborhood or in academic or professional circles (Aries and Libra are both cardinal signs). But his feeling of self-importance also lies in the field of communication, in that of collaboration with others, which can give him a great deal of energy (in combination with Sun in Aries). On the other hand, this factor lends itself so readily to rivalry that it can evoke feelings of insecurity. This disturbs his need for comfort and safety in his surroundings, and can also have an unsettling effect on his desire to share common ideas and ideals (Venus in Aquarius) and his sensitivity to atmospheres, which is such that his powers of expression (Mercury) suffer when there is any disruption—disruption for which he, with his Mars in Libra, can be responsible.

In one way or another, the placement of his planets bestows a fundamental duality. Freedom and security oppose one another, as may be seen in the most divergent matters: the need for a place of safety in which to "open up" versus the need to compete and to prove himself on the social scene (Venus in Aquarius and Mercury in Pisces versus Mars in Libra and the Sun in Aries). If he has caused any disturbances he will, under the influence of the same Mars in Libra, take active steps to put matters right, but probably with indifferent success since Mars in Libra plus the Sun in Aries puts too much emphasis on individuality. As soon as he has an uncomfortable sense of insecurity again, the mechanism of the Moon in Taurus switches on automatically to steer his boat back into calmer waters. But at the very moment when everything is going without a hitch and there is nothing to worry about, the Sun in Aries needs some new impulse, or Mars in Libra does something daring; the roundabout starts up all over again. In fact the process is endless.

Jupiter as the need for expansion works mainly on the mind with the planet in Aquarius, and here it serves to strengthen Peter's convictions. Once he has made up his mind on a subject, he listens only to himself, especially where he identifies emotionally with the ideas and ideals to which he has become attached. Jupiter can provide reinforcement in the sense that when he has ideals he can share with others, he can devote himself to them so wholeheartedly that his comrades can put up with his uncertainties, fickleness and restlessness for the sake of the good he does. But, by the same token, he will give himself to something utterly worthless and, in spite of the fact that as an Aries he is not unduly worried about finishing things, will with the assistance of his Moon in Taurus and Jupiter in Aquarius persist in his course of action with great determination.

Although his Saturn, the factor that demarcates the ego and gives a feeling of responsibility, is operating from the inferior element, this does not mean that Peter is unable to form an ego or that he has no sense of responsibility. One has only to talk with him to realize that he is perfectly capable of undertaking tasks and of seeing them through to completion. But conventional obligations make little sense to him and this can land him in difficulties from time to time. Notwithstanding the helpfulness inherent in Saturn in Virgo, Peter has problems with being helpful. He is often obliging and willing to be of assistance, but only when it suits *him*. He has difficulty in learning to see that his help may be important on occasions which are not so convenient.

This same Saturn in Virgo, which is so apt at analyzing and studying humanity, can eventually bring him face to face with himself when he has learned to accept a number of responsibilities, and, with his Jupiter in Aquarius and his Sun in Aries, he will be honest enought to acknowledge the things mentioned and will try to shape up accordingly. Mercury is something of a problem here because, being posited in such an emotional sign (Pisces), it makes it hard for him to view matters objectively. His objectivity is endangered by the unrealistic way in which he sometimes looks at himself.

Peter has a need for emotional experiences, for mental contacts, for freedom and security and, in short, for a whole range of conflicting possibilities, from among which it is hard for him to choose. The possibilities struggle with one another and it is not easy to say which will come out on top. So Peter will go through many phases before he gets the contradictory features of his character into perspective. Quite apart from the aspects and other interpretative data, the planets in the signs of Peter's birth chart display plenty of tension, and suggest a life filled with contradictions and conflicts. This can make Peter very versatile, but there is a real risk that he may end up as a dilettante. He will need to watch out for this.

SUMMARY OF
THE PLANETS, ELEMENTS
AND CROSSES

The meanings of the planets, elements and crosses have already been fully disscussed in Volume 1 of this series. A quick review will probably be useful to the reader who wishes to try combining the various factors in a chart. This section provides a quick look at the planets and components which go to make up the signs (*i.e.*, the elements and crosses).

1. THE PLANETS

THE SUN

Keynotes: the ego, the best way to go to develop in accordance with one's inmost desires.

Innate drive: to be and to realize oneself. The Sun has an integrating function in the psyche and, as such, represents how we try to integrate the other factors in our psyche.

Placement tells us something about how an individual tries to achieve his or her goals and ideals.

Possible modes of expression: vitality and creative urge, dynamism, warmth, vitality, actual creativity and energy. Self-confidence, willpower, leadership. Ambition, lust for power, striving for power, egocentricity, ostentation and boastfulness, despotism. Timidity, inadequacy or lack of ambition. Organization.

THE MOON

Keynotes: the subliminal emotional life, unconsciously acquired habits, reproduction, reflection.

Innate drive: the urge to reproduce the creative principle of the Sun in a wealth of different forms.

Placement tells us something about how the individual expresses his unconscious reactions. The behavior adopted by people when their circumstances make them unsure; their methods of making themselves feel more at ease. Conditioned and socially acceptable behavior (the mask). The unthinking reaction pattern.

Possible modes of expression: form-giving creativity, imagination, amenableness, receptivity, reproduction, mimicry, fickleness, easily roused feelings, emotionalism, sensitivity, restlessness. Invention, adaptability, sympathy, productivity, delving into the past, caution, retention of impressions. Cherishing, providing, mothering and protecting. Instability, uncertainty, unreliability, fondness of one's relations, weak will, apathetic behavior, emotional outbursts, shamming.

MERCURY

Keynotes: analysis, arranging, classification, contemplation, exchanging and communicating in a neutral manner.

Innate drive: the urge to classify the experiences and phenomena of life, to sort, study and analyze them with a view to assimilation; the desire to recognize and assimilate unconscious motives by conscious meditation and analysis, and by seeing oneself in others (contacts).

Placement tells us something about how we sort out and assimilate our experiences and factual data, the way in which we think, communicate and make contacts.

Possible modes of expression: thinking, linking the conscious with the unconscious, bring people together, connecting facts and events.

Analysis, the need to gather and classify information. Communication, eloquence, desire for knowledge, interest in new theories, (ultra-) critical attitude, cunning, inconstancy, unreliability and garrulousness. Restlessness, quick-wittedness in debates, forgetfulness, irritability, irresolution, nervousness.

VENUS

Keynotes: the need for comfort and safety in emotional and material things, an appreciation of harmony and beauty, the passive form of the instinct for self-preservation.

Innate drive: the desire to unite opposites and to bring them into a state of balance and permanent harmony.

Placement tells us something about the way in which we value the life of the emotions, how we react emotionally in our relationships, and how we look for security on the emotional and material plane.

Possible modes of expression: creating harmony, making peace, arriving at compromises, forming relationships and friendships, uniting opposites. Collaboration, partnership, poise, sympathy, peaceableness, artistry, a feeling for esthetics and beauty, love, affection. Slovenliness, awkwardness (clumsiness), lack of tact, laziness, immorality, vanity. Bashfulness.

MARS

Keynotes: aggressive form of the instinct for self-preservation, the wish to prove oneself, executive power, energy.

Innate drive: the urge to set oneself apart from others or from a group, to emphasize one's own individuality and to prove one's worth.

Placement tells us something about how the individual uses his energy and makes his presence felt.

Possible modes of expression: aggression, executive ability, vying with others, self-assertion, ambition, pugnacity, setting oneself against others. Ardent desires, strong personal involvement in events, fierceness, sexuality, absurd behavior, adverturousness, dissoluteness, independence, lack of restraint, courage, readiness to take risks, pioneering spirit, love of action, spontaneity, competitiveness and love of conquest. Recklessness, impudence, egotism, passion, destructiveness, violence, coarseness, vehemence, power madness, intolerance.

JUPITER

Keynotes: spiritual and religious needs, extension, propagation and expansion.

Innate drive: the desire to view facts and events within a wider framework; to propagate, to bring about an increase and improvement in spirit and in matter.

Placement tells us something about how we experience spiritual and religious needs, the way in which we give shape to the principle of expansion in us, or the way in which we try to feed our inner and outer growth.

Possible modes of expression: growth of consciousness and insight, increase in knowledge and understanding, the formation of spiritual and religious norms and values, growth and expansion, the propagation of one's own insights, improving one's status. Justice, generosity, leniency, magnanimity. Protectiveness, religious belief, love of healing, preservation. Obtrusive helpfulness, snobbishness. Liberty Hall, lawlessness, self-righteousness, arrogance, overestimation of self, rashness, extravagance, hypocrisy. Fanaticism. Mental journeys (studying, etc.), as well as journeys in the flesh (trips abroad) to widen one's horizons. Philosophical and pedagogical leanings. The ability to understand the larger issues. Good judgment. Optimism.

SATURN

Keynotes: the formation of consciousness; learning through pain; the ultimate form and structure; our limitations.

Innate drive: the desire for ego development, penetration to the kernel of things, development of a sense of personal responsibility. The desire to find one's own limits in testing conditions.

Placement tells us something about the vulnerable spot in our characters and about the way we mold them in the face of disappointment and suffering.

Possible modes of expression: self-respect, ambition, the wish to supply good work, the need to function adequately. Concentrated energy, goal orientation, tenacity, the wish to consolidate, the passing of laws and decrees, regulation, control. Demarcation, limitation, restriction, realistic and practical attitude to life. Learning from one's mistakes, introspection, sobriety, fidelity, patience. Fear, pessimism, retirement, grief, trouble, care. Loneliness, isolation, inadequacy, abandoment. Protection mechanisms, prohibitions. Seriousness, capability, diligence, perseverence, sense of duty, distrust, fatalism, pettiness, heartlessness, inflexibility, coolness. Insecurity, responsibility.

URANUS

Keynotes: independence and originality. Breaking of form and crossing established boundaries.

Innate drive: the urge to develop a distinctive and original individuality and identity. The wish to be oneself. The unconscious urge to make changes, to sever relationships, to break through barriers.

Placement shows the way in which we seek to express and develop our own individuality.

Possible modes of expression: originality, uniqueness, independence, flashing and brilliant ideas, individual creativity, rebelliousness, overthrowing the existing order, anarchy, destructiveness. Freedom, joyfulness, fraternity. Self-improvement and self-expression. Eccentricity, explosive behavior, capriciousness, violence, impulsiveness. Tolerance, spiritual interests, fascination with the occult.

NEPTUNE

Keynotes: the dissolving and attenuation of form; blurred outlines, idealizing, making improvements.

Innate drive: the desire to refine existing psychic factors and to tune into cosmic values. Treating the everyday world as an impersonal or depersonalized ideal.

Placement says something about the way in which one experiences higher spiritual values, but also about the way in which it is possible to become befogged or to build castles in the air. The way in which a person expresses universal love.

Possible modes of expression: refinement, sensing untold depths in the world of experience, universal love, understanding, warmth, dedication to humanity. The source of inspiration for religion and art. Idealization and empathy. Rich powers of imagery, great sensitivity, strong susceptibility. Flight from everyday realities, daydreaming, hallucinations, unreal and pseudoreligious experiences. Patient self-denial, obsession, irrational fears, instability, escapism, bemused thinking, deception of self and others, hysteria. Formlessness or transcendence of form. The wedding of thought to feeling. Reveries, rich fantasies, looking at everything through rose-colored spectacles, illusions, the distortion of objective fact. Seeing things indistinctly, or losing one's mental track in a mist, but also: spiritual expansion and the experience of universal spiritual values. Love of humanity, subtlety, romanticism, tenderness, sensitivity, mysticism. Fine appearances, glamour, ecstatic and strange experiences, addictions. Transcendence of or liquidation of the personality.

PLUTO

Keynotes: the will to power, the bringing to the surface of submerged unconscious factors. Transcendence of form.

Innate drive: the inner urge to liquidate or to transform the resurrected unconscious factors in order to be able to assimilate and integrate them and to create a balance between the conscious and the unconscious.

Placement shows the form taken by the compulsive urge to achieve integration, the direction of the will processes and power complexes, and how the transformation processes operate.

Possible modes of expression: heavily emotional, hysterical, volcanic outbursts, sudden severe shocks, tensions, neurotic tendencies, danger that the psyche will be shattered by unconscious disturbances and that the ego will be crushed, manna personality, power complexes. The wish to penetrate into psychic mechanisms. Self-destruction, but also the power to "die to be reborn" after metamorphosis; the desire for continuous renewal. Manipulation, reformation. Psychic powers, the use of concentrated willpower.

2. THE ELEMENTS

The elements reveal the way in which we regard the world of phenomena and focus our minds on it. We recognize four basic attitudes, corresponding to the four "elements": fire, earth, air and water. These represent the four fundamental manners of experiencing a given part of the whole:

1. Earth or perception first looks at the object in respect of its constituent parts, its form, its materials and its quality;

2. air or thinking places the facts within a conceptual framework or theory and links the facts together;

3. water or feeling imparts to the whole a certain emotional value, while

4. fire or intuition looks at the whole in terms of its possibilities and future, penetrating so to speak behind the material form to more recondite factors.

Since the elements create the background from which we experience and view the world of phenomena, they must also form the backgrounds out of which the influences of the planets develop. Thus the manner in which a planet brings its influence to bear depends on the mode of expression represented by the element in which it happens to be placed. (However, the role played by the said planet in the assimilation processes of the psyche is given by the crosses.)

FIRE

Attitude: seeking for the phenomena *behind* matter; the question of the why of things. Where does a phenomenon come from and how will it further develop? Looking for the connection, the subtle link that binds everything together underneath the surface. The unconscious and intuitive components of events.

Behavior: self-orientated, enthusiastic, optimistic, full of confidence, naive, impulsive, creative, inspiring, forward looking, spontaneous, warm, loyal, honest, self-assertive, original, enthusiastic, but also: obtrusive, rash, irresponsible, extravagant, careless, ambitious, impatient, immoderate, hasty, prone to make a drama out of things, masterful.

Possibilities: displaying unquenchable activity; violent action; sharp reactions, courage, energetic and inspiring activities. Displaying ideal perseverence without much anxiety; the freebooter who lives by a moral code of his own while asserting his right to freedom; unprejudiced openness to all kinds of fresh options; a need for change. The ability to gain deep, and sometimes prophetic, insights.

Difficulties: finding it hard to listen to others; obstinately defending one's own position; lack of self-control; tactlessness; difficulty in giving shape to perceptions. Under- and sometimes overvaluation of material things and values. A compulsive, unconscious bond with the material world. Helplessness. Quickness to be taken up with unreal things and a tendency to lose sight of reality. The risk of complete physical or spiritual exhaustion.

EARTH

Attitude: concentrated on perceptible reality and on the construction of material security. Very much involved with the five senses. Geared to concrete and material form and on their quality and structure.

Behavior: practical, solid, reliable, diligent, patient, prudent, self-possessed, passive, dependent, tenacious, conventional, formal, efficient, unassuming, obliging, tolerant, purposeful, dogged, concentrated, sober, reserved. Also: obstinate, stiff, without initiative, suspicious, unsure, indolent, slow, superstitious, clinging to outworn ethics.

Possibilities: devotion to scientific research with the necessary perseverence and practical understanding. Developing activities efficiently and without waste. Shaping things with a feeling for form and material. Looking at the facts in a down-to-earth manner. Having a sensual and hedonistic attitude to form, including that of the body; artistry.

Difficulties: taking motivation and inspiration from others; a practical attitude which can get bogged down in minutiae; excessive emphasis on physical and material externals and on enjoyment and sensuality. Rootedness in possessions in order to have something to cling to; fear of change and preference for familiar routines. Incapacity for abstract and/or theoretical thought.

AIR

Attitude: largely concerned with forging links between people, events and so on from a rational point of view. Interest in communication and exchange.

Behavior: emphasis on the social aspects of life; objective, peace loving, active and industrious, animated, studious, communicative, theorizing, logical, harmonious, friendly, liberal. Also: lack of firmness, lack of continuity, changeable, cool, unemotional, impersonal, dualistic, opinionated and dogmatic.

Possibilities: thinking in abstract forms, in ideas and concepts makes possible the formulation and elaboration of (involved) theories, helped by liveliness of mind. Intellectual capacity, flexibility in thought, word and gesture. The thinking processes are central, and there is a liking for discussion. Testing things by the laws of logic. Constructive thinking that can "fly high."

Difficulties: rationalization of the emotions through overemphasis on reason with a corresponding reduction in spontaneity. The risk of rigid formalization, and that reliance on theory will lead to a loss of touch with reality. Letting one's thoughts run away with one to the point of fanaticism, and aversion to criticism. Losing sight of reality so that too little attention is paid to material things, and sometimes to the body itself.

WATER

Attitude: investing people, things, events, etc. with an emotional value; the emotional evaluation of life.

Behavior: sensitive, relying on feelings, vulnerable, easily influenced, amenable, retiring, peace loving, sympathetic, engaging, amiable, protective, inquisitive, eager, expectant, altruistic, deeply emotional. But also: unstable, passive, oversensitive, uncertain, sentimental, emotionally possessive, suspicious, watchful, mistrustful, covetous, greedy, liable to "fall apart," insincere, inconstant, imperious, domineering, intriguing.

Possibilities: the ability to give a long-term care and protection due to great reserves of unconscious strength; an understanding of human nature; lovingness. The ability to get to the core of things and to develop unconscious wisdom through the cultivation of quiet, through hidden psychic and/or occult powers, and through a great capacity for absorbing and resolving the facts of experience. A strong reaction to atmospheres.

Difficulties: problems with logical thought; problems over acquiring a personal identity due to a ready identification with others; unconscious egoism. Oppressive presence, tyranny. Behind a childlike and banal mask, and an apparent unconcern and emotional coldness, there often lies a welter of satisfactions and dissatisfactions. Willingness to be molded by others, even to the point of suffering.

3. THE CROSSES

The contents of the psyche are bound together by streams of psychic energy. This makes possible a constant process of assimilation. The crosses symbolize the manner in which the individual assimilates and integrates his or her experiences. The three crosses guide the processes, each in its own way, and each have their own mode of adapting to external and internal circumstances and changes. The cardinal cross is mainly toward the inside world, and the mutable cross hovers between the two: the direction taken by this cross depends on the mood of the moment.

THE CARDINAL CROSS

Orientation: to the conscious needs of life and the environment. Willingness to meet the demands of everyday life.

Psychological aspect: a continual development and differentiation of the superior element. Consciousness has a certain degree of involvement with its own development. Conformity to external values. Need to experience "give-and-take" with the outside world. The urge to make one's presence felt. Subjective factors are often undervalued owing to an undue readiness to compromise over the various factors in one's own nature. A risk that consciousness will be overemphasized at the expense of the unconscious mind.

Signs: Aries, Cancer, Libra, Capricorn.

THE FIXED CROSS

Orientation: to internal, personal needs slumbering in the unconscious. Listening to the inner voice.

Psychological aspect: the regressive flow of the life energy.

Characteristics: activation of the inferior function. The ability to bring a too heavily weighted consciousness back in balance with the rest of the psyche. Intensification of psychic contents which have previously been thrust into the background or even suppressed. No conscious interest in the development of consciousness alone. The psychic energy tends to take a "natural course," even though this may sometimes present difficulties. Because of factors disturbing to the conscious mind, the fixed cross can sometimes prove "critical" and produce uncertainty. Everything is sought within, and the outer world plays a subordinate role.

Signs: Taurus, Leo, Scorpio, Aquarius.

THE MUTABLE CROSS

Orientation: both to the demands of the environment and to the inner demands of the unconscious, depending on the situation at the time. Sometimes absolutely no clear-cut orientation, or else the native makes up his or her mind after the event.

Psychological aspect: no fixed direction of flow of the life energy. The mutable cross can express itself both progessively and regressively, but can also stand stock still on the border between consciousness and unconsciousness.

Characteristics: making transitions (including the transition between conscious and unconscious, and from progression to regression and the reverse). Duality: can be stimulating and adaptable, but can also put the damper on things. Problem solving, integrating, introducing changes, but with the risk that the process will become an end in itself and that nothing will really be deeply assimilated (such as would happen with the fixed cross) or that consciousness will function properly in the outer world (as the cardinal cross helps it to do). The uniting of opposites, serviceableness, moveableness. The longing for change.

Signs: Gemini, Virgo, Sagittarius, Pisces.

INDEX

cardinal air
Libra, 100
cardinal earth
Capricorn, 78
cardinal fire
Aries, 29
cardinal water
Cancer, 123
consciousness
center of, 2
crisis, 15
Leo, 40
crosses
cardinal, 194
fixed, 195
mutable, 195

E

earth, 192
ego, 8, 14, 15
demarcation of, 13
ego-consciousness
evolution of, 9
element
superior versus inferior, 159
elements, 29, 61, 89, 123, 191

F

feeling function, 134
fire, 191
fixed air
Aquarius, 110
fixed earth
Taurus, 61
fixed fire
Leo, 39

fixed water
Scorpio, 134
Fred's chart, 173, 174

G

Gemini
Jupiter in, 97
Mars in, 95
Mercury in, 93
Moon in, 24, 91
Neptune in, 99
Pluto in, 99
Saturn in, 98
Sun in, 24, 89
Uranus in, 99
Venus in, 94
Great Mother, 9
group members, 5

H

Harding, M. E., 2
healing power, 164

I

individual, 5, 10, 11
inferior function, 135, 161
initiation ceremonies, 9
insecurity, 137
interpretation, 24
introjection, 13

J

Jung, C. G., 16
Jupiter, 8, 9, 10, 26, 36, 47, 56, 67,
76, 85, 97, 107, 119, 131, 142,
155, 164, 165, 188

BIBLIOGRAPHY

Berg, Prof. Dr. J. H. van den. *Metabletica of Leer der Veranderingen* [The Fundamentals of a Historical Psychology]. Nijkirk: 1970.

Hamaker-Zondag, K. M. *Aspects & Personality*. York Beach, ME: Samuel Weiser, 1990.

————. *Foundations of Personality*. York Beach, ME: Samuel Weiser, 1994. Combines *Elements & Crosses as the Basis of the Horoscope* and *Houses and Personality Development* into one volume.

————. *Handbook of Horary Astrology*. York Beach, ME: Samuel Weiser, 1992.

————. *The House Connection*. York Beach, ME: Samuel Weiser, 1994.

————. *Psychological Astrology: Astrological Symbolism & the Human Psyche*. York Beach, ME: Samuel Weiser, 1989. Formerly *Astro-Psychology*. York Beach, ME: Samuel Weiser, and Wellingborough, UK: The Aquarian Press, 1980.

————. *The Twelfth House*. York Beach, ME: Samuel Weiser, 1992.

Harding, M. E. *The I and the Not I: A Study in the Development of Consciousness*. Princeton, NJ: Princeton University Press, 1973.

Kühr, E. C. *Psychologische Horoskopdeutung: Analyse und Synthese, Vol. 1*. Vienna: 1948.

Neumann, E. *The Origins and History of Consciousness*. Princeton, NJ: Princeton University Press, 1969.

Karen Hamaker-Zondag started her astrological practice in 1975. She is a founding member of two schools in Holland: an astrological school, Stichting Achernar, and a school of Jungian psychology, Stichting Odrerir, with a current enrollment of over 200 students. She is a graduate of the University of Amsterdam with doctoral degrees in social geography and environmental engineering. Her post-graduate study of psychology, astrology, and parapsychology inspired a full-time counseling practice. A leading astrologer in Holland, she publishes a quarterly astrological journal, *Symbolon*, with her husband Hans. She lectures extensively throughout the world, traveling to Russia, Japan, Canada, the USA, and all over Europe, where she has been enthusiastically received by the astrological communtiy. She has written thirteen books including *Aspects and Personality, Foundations of Personality, Handbook of Horary Astrology, The House Connection, Psychological Astrology*, and *The Twelfth House*, all published by Samuel Weiser.